NEW EDINBURGH REVIEW ANTHOLOGY

Edited by
JAMES CAMPBELL

POLYGON BOOKS

ISBN 0 904919 56 0

First published 1982 by
Polygon Books,
1 Buccleuch Place,
Edinburgh, EH8 9LW.

Reproduced from copy supplied, printed and bound by
Spectrum Printing Company,
10-24 Burlington Street,
Edinburgh, EH6 5JH.

*The publisher acknowledges subsidy from the
Scottish Arts Council towards the
publication of this volume.*

CONTENTS

CONTENTS [contd.]

James Campbell

INTRODUCTION

ONE of the complaints most often heard in literary
Scotland today is of the lack of a political and cultural
weekly along the lines of the *New Statesman* and the *Spectator*.
There is in fact no regular journal, enjoying the luxury of
weekly publication which allows a cooler view than that
usually taken by the daily newspapers, whose responsibility it
is to digest, discuss and, possibly, influence progress and
change in every hole and corner of society as it is seen to
happen; no paper which can make available to political
commentators and *littérateurs* the space and freedom to write
at length about developments in architecture, economics,
literature, psychology — all the cultural activities, central and
peripheral, which affect our daily lives in ways sometimes
invisible, often all too visible, which it is the duty of the poet
and the critic to explain.

Indeed it is likely that there cannot be such a journal in
Scotland, just as there cannot be profound social change, until
there is real political activity. If one were inclined to
revolutionary methods, Hugh MacDiarmid once remarked,
one could never find in Scotland a person worth killing, in the
sense of that person possessing political power and therefore
needing to be got rid of. Scotland has no politics, no seat of
power, so what on earth would a Scottish *New Statesman* or
Spectator find to fill its columns with week after week?

From time to time the attempt to satisfy this complaint
results in the establishment of a magazine whose brave
appearance in the world is heralded in one quarter by

1

unfounded optimism, in another by groans of "we've seen it all before", and in yet another, worst of all, by total neglect. If it runs true to form, the new review starts life as a weekly, but soon afterwards (after unforeseeably skipping an issue or two, or appearing on Monday or Tuesday instead of Friday) announces the change to fortnightly issue, which dismays the readership because they can never remember which weekend it will be coming out and which not (and weeklies gain a large part of their sales by habitual purchase) so that it is soon forced to slow down further and become a monthly, before finally lying down and gasping — in vain — for breath. The most poignant repeat of this pattern recently was the journal which began by calling itself *7 Days*.

The people behind these undernourished creatures are rarely motivated by less than the highest principles: they spend a lot of time, and often money, trying to make the child walk and talk by itself; but altruism on the part of the parents is not enough to give a bairn the will to live. The relation of cultural journalism to politics is such that a weekly journal of arts and affairs finds it impossible to exist long enough in Scotland for it to be able to gain a large readership, which will tempt advertisers, which will provide sufficient capital to pay good writers, which in turn would expand the enterprise and scope of the journal.

What Scotland (in particular Edinburgh) does have is a proliferation of small magazines, appearing quarterly or less. At any time there may be as many as fifteen of these curious, little-read, scraggy beings in the capital city alone (it should be remembered too that Edinburgh is a city roughly one-twentieth of the size of modern London) being sold in pubs or to contributors' friends; without pausing to think hard I can number twenty-five such publications in existence now or else at some time during the four years in which I edited the *New Edinburgh Review*. This does not count the magazine which most Scots literati regard as the apotheosis of this sort of journal of arts and affairs: not an equivalent of the weekly *New Statesman* but a quarterly, subsequently a monthly, with a strong emphasis on literature: *Scottish International.*

Scottish International was an excellent magazine, in a tradition of periodicals issuing from Scotland which fail to survive partly because they are inevitably regarded as "provincial" by critics based in London, most parochial of all cities, but more because of indifference on the part of the Scottish reading public. Before *Scottish International*, during the 1950s, there was *Saltire Review*, another good magazine which came out quite happily for several years as a quarterly, before changing to monthly, and expiring. Before that there was *The Modern Scot*, also a quarterly, edited by J. H. Whyte and described by Edwin Muir in 1934 as "the best literary review that has appeared in Scotland for many decades, [which] has now maintained for several years a critical standard which is unique there".

No Scottish writer of this century has been as conscious as Muir was of the function of the periodical within a national literature, nor has anyone stated so positively the need for such an organ in Scotland. The creation of *The Modern Scot*, however, did not inspire real optimism in him, although he encouraged it and contributed to it. A few years earlier, in a letter to Whyte, he had made plain his feelings about the plight of Scottish literature, and even forecast its eventual disappearance.

> How long it will take for this to happen it is impossible to say — a few centuries, or only one, what does it matter? "Hugh MacDiarmid" will become a figure like Burns — an exceptional case, that is to say — an arbitrary apparition of the national genius, robbed of his legitimate effect because there will be no literary tradition to perpetuate it.... All this, looked at from outside might almost make us imagine that Scotland's historical destiny is to eliminate itself in reality, as it has already wellnigh eliminated itself from history and literature — the forms in which a nation survives.

But in spite of his pessimism, Muir would have admitted that Whyte's endeavour in producing *The Modern Scot* was an

3

expression of faith, the effects of which, however short-lived, could only be beneficial to the national literature. Magazines like it, including those mentioned, have a valuable purpose in publishing the work of young writers at what may be a crucial stage in their careers, and also in procuring writing by established authors, not only to raise the tone of the company and make potential customers reach for their pockets, but also to demonstrate simply that the publication in Scotland of writers of international renown is a matter of concern to Scots.

In Scotland the little magazines* have the function — though not the potential audience — of the weeklies, hence their importance. Not only do they encourage new writers, but often they have the opportunity to devote several pages (sadly uncluttered by advertising) to a book or a topic to which the national daily newspapers might be able to give only a column. Moreover, in spite of their limited circulation, they have a permanence which the daily and weekly papers have not: a writer will reach more people and receive higher payment by writing in a Sunday newspaper than in the *London Magazine*, but almost everyone who buys the latter keeps it, it is stored in libraries, frequently referred to, and articles from it are often reprinted in other places.

Depending on what your interest is, the survival of little magazines is a matter of indifference, puzzlement or great wonder. They always cater for limited, sometimes tiny, audiences — T. S. Eliot's *Criterion* had a circulation of roughly 400 — which even when relatively large are not big enough to finance the payment to contributors of fees proportionate to the time, effort and skill which goes into the creation of an essay or even a book review, never mind a poem. They are, in a sense, born failures. The most famous (and possibly the best) little magazine to have existed in Britain this century, Cyril Connolly's *Horizon*, never sold more than 5,000, something

---

* The term "little magazine" is of uncertain origin, but may derive from the name of the *Little Review*, edited by Jane Heap and Margaret Anderson, where among much other fine material, portions of Joyce's *Ulysses* were first published.

which eventually sickened the editor and caused the closure of the magazine.

No editor, of even the smallest magazine, will have difficulty in recognising the pattern which begins with the indifference of libraries asked to take out a subscription, the unwillingness of wholesalers to stock anything which doesn't show a nude riding a motorbike on the cover, the curious reluctance of even those who profess to consider such magazines a good thing to pay for the privilege of seeing it survive, leading to the labour and cost and, finally, the exhaustion of constantly resuscitating the faint subscription list. Still, with careful attention to literary standards, with an unlimited devotion from a low-paid (or unpaid) staff of three or two or one, and with some financial assistance, they survive long enough to make an impression on the culture which gave them birth and with which they have necessarily maintained a tense love-hate relationship.

Editors of literary magazines, in Scotland as elsewhere, have a clear duty to seek out and publish new talent, but the critical function of a magazine is of almost equal importance. A magazine provides the forum where the business of criticism may proceed as in a debate, and the more outspoken that criticism sounds the better it will serve to mitigate Muir's gloomy prognosis of ultimate decline. However, critics in Scotland are more in danger of being kind to be cruel than in most other places, partly out of concern not to wound and partly from a fear of giving offence to someone they are likely to meet at the next cocktail party: which leads one to the inevitable conclusion that they are putting cocktail parties before literature — not as preposterous a notion as it first sounds. Without a critical atmosphere in which it is possible to speak out against the work of friends as well as adversaries, there will be no literature worth speaking of at all, or, worse, worth reading.

The fostering of an indigenous Scottish literature is, of course, of primary importance, but the Scottish writer finds himself in the dilemma of not knowing whether he is expected to stay close to the hearth and nurse the family traditions, or to leave home and look outwards — to Europe, America and England, most obviously. It seems to me that the latter is the healthier response, from editors as well as writers: to pretend that Scottish literature can attain the richness of tradition revealed in English or French or German literatures can only lead deeper and deeper into the kind of chauvinism which substitutes sentimentality for feeling and prejudice for discrimination.

There are many good critics at work in Scotland today (most of whom have, I hope, been asked at least once to write for the *New Edinburgh Review*) yet there is no more a coherent idea of critical standards in the country now than there was when Muir wrote his pessimistic letter to Whyte in 1931. The critical reception of a book is still influenced by the context of its creation to an unhealthy degree. Different standards apply for writing done by Scots than for writing by others. When the critic of *The Scotsman* reviewed the annual *Scottish Short Stories* in 1980, she began by praising two of the book's items and then wrote that "it would be invidious to make qualitative judgements about the other writers" included in the anthology. This critic should have been able to see that it did the writers under review no service at all to suggest that they were beneath criticism. The response is, unfortunately, a common one and far from encouraging the potential in our literature, it can only hasten its elimination.

* * *

The *New Edinburgh Review* was founded in 1969 by a group of students, only a few doors away from the house where, over a century and a half before, the *Edinburgh Review* was founded by three young Whig lawyers. During the years since its creation, the *New Edinburgh Review* has passed through many forms, had modest successes and dismal failures, and even (like all true adventurers) come close to death. Among the people who have had a hand in its fortunes in the past are Owen

Dudley Edwards, Tom Nairn, Hamish Henderson, Paul Atkinson and the late Robert Garioch, who for many years acted as poetry editor.

One of the past editors of the *New Edinburgh Review* offered as his reason for quitting after three issues that "only a masochist would remain for longer, and not even anyone among my legions of enemies has yet accused me of being a masochist".

So far as I know, my own reputation is similarly unstained, despite the fact that I managed to endure more than three of these, apparently, flagellatory experiences. There were, no doubt, a number of reasons for doing so, and one of them was the conviction that the dissociative personality of the *New Edinburgh Review* in the past suggested that what it needed most was someone prepared to stick around longer than any other editor had done so far; someone who would attempt to give the magazine something of what is called "identity".

The simplest way of achieving this is to centre the editorial activity around a cause. With this in mind as their *raison d'être*, editors new to magazines often come equipped with a "policy" which, they believe, will give direction to the vehicle. Magazines of this sort have a shorter life expectancy than other journals (because, I suppose, they speak to the converted), although often their existence has been a worthwhile one. Sometimes the occasion demanded the creation of a magazine devoted to this or that particular cause, but more often it happens that the person in charge has a drum to beat and has found, at last, a place to do so.

It was my decision to jettison the "causes" with which the *New Edinburgh Review* had previously (sometimes remotely) been connected, and also to jettison the practice of basing a whole issue — often a so-called "double-issue" — around a theme. Theme issues, of whatever magazine, often fill a genuine gap, but more often they are the result of a personal crusade, or of laziness. The main objection to them is that they contradict the idea of a *magazine*, resembling more a book of essays in magazine shape. It seemed to me that what we needed most in Scotland was a journal which would do what it could to attend to all forms of cultural activity, treating each as seriously as possible, without spreading the jam too thinly — always a danger in a journal which appears only four times a year.

There seems to be an assumption that a magazine devoting most of its attention to the arts cannot exist in Scotland without self-consciously proclaiming its Scottishness. Writers, readers, shopkeepers and other interested parties seem to expect this, even to encourage it, and yet the cry of "parochialism!" is ringing forever in our ears. If a magazine devotes more space to things Scottish than anything else, then it is immediately in danger of being branded parochial. But if, like the *Literary Review*, during the time that it was edited from Edinburgh, it spends no more space on Scottish affairs than on any other, then along comes the complaint that it is being neglectful.

Can we have it both ways? Can we pursue and reflect what interests us most, regardless of creed or flag, and still not lose sight of the responsibility which comes with being a journal of arts and affairs based in Scotland? It appeared to me that we could, and my editorial policy at the moment of taking office was directed by no causes, no cliques, no right or left, schools of thought, or any method of approach which might be deemed exclusive. Above all, not the promotion of "Scottish-ness" above general excellence, or as a substitute for intelligence. My concern then, as now, was for good writing, and my policy nothing other than trying to foster a feeling for language and a sense of style, applied to a variety of genres. Out of that alchemy is bound to emerge some valuable material.

The contents of this anthology cannot be said truthfully to represent "the best of the *New Edinburgh Review*". Far too many good writers have given generously of their talents for that to be possible in a single volume. In making the selection I have adhered to quite simple criteria, choosing on the whole, and I suppose naturally, what I liked best. There were several outstanding articles which served their purpose at the time but did not lend themselves to reprinting. Three of the pieces here began life as book reviews, but it seemed wise to favour those essays which came to exist independently of the book. Moreover, in editing an issue of a magazine an editor has the task—and he relies largely on his instinct in fulfilling it—of "orchestrating" the contents, getting the balance right: a principle which also had to rule the selection for this book. So, of two excellent pieces on related subjects, only one could be allowed to pass.

There were several which simply could not be resisted. To mention only a few: Don Watson's biographical study of a ruthless Scots pioneer in Australia; Douglas Dunn's timely examination of MacDiarmid's excesses before the "age of MacDiarmid" had a greater span in fantasy than in reality (wha's like us in committing this kind of sin?); Rick Cluchey's account of his relationship with Samuel Beckett and Naomi Mitchison's portrait of her father. In the fiction department, there are stories by three lesser known authors which would be unembarrassed in any company, and by George Mackay Brown an example of his art at its finest.

It would also have been difficult to pass over the essay by James Baldwin, the "story" by Henry Miller, and the neat note to his first novel by John Fowles. Baldwin agreed to do the piece on jazz when this editor had produced only two issues and, looking back, the evidence was not especially promising. He accepted the offer to write for no other reason than that he was offered a subject about which he had something to say which he had not yet said. That he decided to do so in a relatively small journal from a country he has never visited is only consistent with his kindness, integrity and willingness to help younger writers. He speaks from a great height — is, as he says in the essay here, "the son of the Preacher-Man".

Some critics have been slow to understand the change of style which has affected Baldwin's later writing since his early success, a change which has its origin in a changed conscious- ness and sense of his duty as a writer. The sentences of "Of the

Sorrow Songs" are not the superb, Jamesian sentences of *The Fire Next Time* and *Notes of Native Son*. By the early 1960s Baldwin had mastered his style and was already acclaimed as the author of some of the most eloquent essays to be written this century. Even by then he had recognised that what was happening to his world and to himself was forcing him to take new directions in syntax.

The circumstances of procuring Henry Miller's "Mother" were rather more orthodox, but the timing of its publication was extraordinary. The brief Prefatory Note explains Miller's inspiration for "Mother": "This text was inspired by a dream in which I died and found myself in Devachan (limbo) where I ran into my mother whom I hated all my life."

It went through the usual stages of production and copies of the issue containing it were in the shops on 6th June 1980. The next day Miller was dead. He would have appreciated the fact that his last published work drew its inspiration from a dream of his own death. It would have appealed to his sense of humour.

My special thanks go to Brian McCabe and Judy Nussbaum, who at different times have given freely of their assistance and enthusiasm in helping to prepare what often seemed to be an endless path paved by the current issue, the next one and the one after that, to James Hutcheson whose natural sense of design enables him to produce front cover artwork of a consistent and unusually high standard, to Mary Hill who saw the book through production, and to all staff at Polygon Books. In the end, an editor's greatest satisfaction comes from encouraging writers, seeing them succeed elsewhere, perhaps begin to prepare a book. It is in that spirit that the more esteemed authors share their talents, and it is for that mainly that literary magazines exist. In a small but unavoidable sense, each new issue of the magazine, as well as this anthology, owes its existence to everyone who has ever contributed to its pages.

Naomi Mitchison

MY FATHER

M Y father John Scott Haldane was born in 1860. I intend
in this sketch to show how his family background and
early thinking relates to scientific thought and knowledge as it
was developing in the latter half of the nineteenth century.

It would have been quite possible for my father and his
brothers to have lapsed into being not very well-off country
gentlemen or at least it would have been possible had they been
English and had their notion of social morality been based on a
rather different aspect of the same nominal religion. As it was
they were brought up to suppose that a good life was also a
diligent life, that one's God-given talents should be used if
possible for the general betterment of humanity in ways
pleasing to God. There was no doubt a Calvinist tinge in this.
Only the elect are saved. Did the Haldane family, without
thinking about it too much, automatically consider themselves
as the elect? A generation earlier a much loved child had died:
in a booklet for believers there is a long description of her
terminal illness and death and no mention of hell-fire. In the
end angels came for her — in her parents' minds.

There were fewer professions to choose from a hundred
years ago than there are now. The obvious four were the Army,
the Navy, the Church and the Bar. In Scotland the last
included not only barristers but Writers to the Signet. There
were also lower forms of law and commerce. In Scotland it
had been possible earlier in the nineteenth century for a
gentleman's son to enter retail trade but probably by the
'eighties this was no longer so. "Business" in its modern sense

of major technology and money manipulation was not known. The word was associated with uncouth and sometimes brutal English Midlanders. It was out of the question. There was another Haldane son, Geordie, who was apparently a very talented violinist in his teens as well as being a much loved child and his parents had faced the almost unheard of possibility that he might actually become a professional musician. But he died of diphtheria at seventeen. They were a very affectionate family; long afterwards my father spoke of his brother Geordie in words of love and loss.

The boys had followed the usual country pursuits; they could ride and shoot and had some understanding of farming and wildlife. In his twenties my father was doing a good deal of estate management, including renting occasional shootings from neighbours, or, I think, letting their own. They had a tutor, Hume Brown, who later became a well-known historian though his historical writing is mostly outdated now. When I was a child "the Professor" used to come often to Cloan where he had his special room and his special place and respect. The one sister, Elizabeth, unusually for the time was educated along with the boys. My grandmother was something of a feminist. Yet it was assumed that Elizabeth (Aunt Bay to me) would sacrifice an independent life in order to look after her mother and the family house.

The boys also had a period of school, the Edinburgh Academy. My father seemed to recollect it mostly for the pleasure of the running war with the town boys. They went on to university. For my father it was first Jena and then Edinburgh. Continental travel was probably easier in those days and not at all impeded by occasional wars and revolutions, nor was a passport necessary. My father was to be a doctor, not perhaps as reputable as the other professions but at least it had been foreseen by Babba the family nurse. It was socially on the up and Edinburgh, though not as good as it had been two generations back, probably had one of the best medical schools in the British Isles. However, it was certainly clear to my father that the teaching methods at Edinburgh

Medical School compared ill with those at Jena. He was refused a degree at Edinburgh and wrote to his mother in July 1883:

After talking the matter over with Professor Ewart I have appealed against the decision of my examiners to a meeting of the medical faculty of the University so that if the decision is confirmed the responsibility may rest as far as possible on the decision of the professors.

From your letter I see that you have quite misunderstood my motives in the matter. I am dissatisfied with the examination simply because with the knowledge of medicine I possess I think that I ought not to have been rejected. I purposely paid little attention to any of the lectures of my examiners as I consider that the present system of working for examinations is one which is doing a great deal of harm in every way. The case of Professor Simpson's lectures is only one very flagrant example of this system. [This was not the Professor Simpson who became so famous as an obstetrician but his nephew, said to be "a voluminous contributor to medical journals and a successful lecturer".]

I think it well that the students themselves should deal with this matter and I am not sorry that circumstances have made it incumbent on me to bring up the matter here in Edinburgh. Intellectual freedom used to prevail in the Edinburgh School of Medicine and I hope that before long it may do so again.

I have both the money and I think the ability to stand against any number of professors in this matter and probably my reputation, such as it is, in philosophy will be of use to me.

With regard to the ethical questions involved in obstetrics I think there need be nothing in these matters which one ought to shrink from. At the same time I think that a man such as Professor Simpson is quite incompetent to deal with such ethical questions. It would certainly be more pleasant were medicine open to women so that they might take charge of obstetrics but as matters stand I think there ought to be nothing in the subject itself which should repel anyone of even the finest feelings. With regard to telling people

about the result of my examination, I have no wish to make
any secret of it.

There is a note on the letter by my grandmother, his mother,
saying: "Ultimately the Edinburgh degree of M.D. was
conferred upon J.S.H., the Senate having seen its mistake."
However, his wrangle with Edinburgh went on for a long time.
In 1889 he writes again: "I don't expect to get out of the
Edinburgh people more than they are compelled to give. After
all it is not to be expected of them after all our feuds and what
Bo [his brother Richard] has said of them. I have no doubt they
judge my essay as impartially as they can but there certainly is
not one of them competent to give an opinion on the subject of
the essay. They haven't even the necessary books in the
University library, which is scandalously neglected." Probably
this refers to an essay on animal heat. The prize was worth £60,
quite a lot in those days.

However, he didn't much care for any of the universities. In
another letter, undated but apparently about a London
University exam, he says: "Tuesday is the last day of my
examination. I was so done up on Thursday that I really don't
know what I may have put in my zoology paper. The more
however one sees of London University the less one cares to
have any connection with it. A false view of life, combined with
an exceedingly plebeian spirit, appears to pervade the whole
place. One has only to come here to learn to appreciate
Edinburgh University, with all its shortcomings. So far as I
myself am concerned I care very little whether I get through or
not now."

Again: "Oxford seems almost as bad as Edinburgh as
regards working for examinations instead of for a subject's
own sake, only it is done on a bigger scale in Oxford ... I feel
rather sick of teaching men who are simply cramming for an
examination and have neither the time nor the inclination to
work in a thorough way at their subject. I think Uncle John
feels the same thing a good deal, though he has much more
trust in examinations than I have. I hope there may be some
way found of giving men honours degrees by theses as in

Germany." This must have been written in the late 'eighties when he was working as a demonstrator with his uncle, Sir John Burden Sanderson, the Regius Professor of Medicine at Oxford.

This shows I think the kind of stubborn beliefs he held. To go back to Edinburgh, one of the things he did was to publish a spoof pamphlet about medical education at Edinburgh accusing it of being unwilling to recognise new ideas. He invented a sham preface by an imaginary graduate of deepest respectability and altogether it was a good early example of the angry young student. There is also a family legend that in the final Viva one of the board whispered the appropriate answer!

He did an intern year at the Royal Infirmary and then came to the next decision. If he had decided to become a practising doctor he could probably have taken a share in a lucrative practice in Edinburgh. Alternatively he could have gone into public health. The medical officers of health had great opportunities and powers in those days. Edinburgh was the first to appoint them and Littlejohn got through essential urban reforms, as did Gardiner in Glasgow and later Wattie in Aberdeen. This side of things was clearly very important; in fact an intelligent person could hardly avoid it. Most of the medical ward patients, especially the poorer ones, had diseases which could be directly attributed to their living conditions. Some were employed in dangerous trades of which there were many. In fact there was, for example, lead poisoning in several major trades, as well as odd and specialised things like glass-blowers' emphysema. Housing in Edinburgh was appalling and epidemics much feared. It was hardly possible to be healthy there. Those who could afford it moved out, at least in summer and autumn.

Even when I was a child twenty years later there was talk about "bad air" and when my father started as a doctor there was considerable uncertainty about the causes of disease. "Germs" were blamed but what were they? Nobody understood why vaccination protected against smallpox. A few obvious carriers were known — plague rats for instance —

but many parasite cycles were still unknown, though they were being worked on. It was the same in botany. (For instance, the fern life cycle had been discovered but even when I was a botany student at Oxford in 1915 it was not taught. Nor did we get much idea of plants as living entities.) Physics was of course pre-Einstein though fairly advanced because it was connected with flourishing heavy industry.

Indeed it was a wonderful period for research and much of this could be done cheaply and relatively easily with such apparatus as anyone could devise and perhaps make for themselves. Much of it must be a clearing away of old myths and words. When people blamed illness on "the drains" what did they mean? Well, by this time my father was a demonstrator in physiology at University College, Dundee. The city of Dundee had a particularly fascinating drainage system in which one might find one's way either by the smell of jute or of marmalade oranges. All his life my father remembered them with a kind of affection. Again I have a letter to his mother, not dated but clearly from the 'eighties.

> We had another turn at the Dundee sewers today. It is very interesting work and one learns a deal by it. The sewers here are much smaller than the ones at Westminster but more interesting. One is getting very expert in disappearing down manholes in the street though I find the Dundee manholes a very tight fit sometimes and had to be pulled up one in which I got stuck. One sewer in which we were on Tuesday smelt quite like an orange grove. It received all the insides of the bitter oranges used at Keiller's marmalade works. The sewer men seem sometimes to have very exciting adventures but do not appear ever to come to any harm. The sewer from Hilltown which comes down a very steep hill with the main sewer seems to be difficult to manage. Even today when there was no rain the roar of the waters coming down sounded very impressive and one could hear it a long way off along the sewer, like the sound of a very large waterfall. We have got to manage very well without

apparatus which one lets down with ropes but it is very difficult to manage when the sewer is less than four feet high, as is often the case.

Remember in those days "bad air" did not only occur inside the drains. It seeped through the elegant town houses of Edinburgh. It was before the days of the now universal U-bend and that in itself led to unwillingness to use the lavatory and consequent constipation and headaches. So the hunt for this bad air was on and what, at the end, was good air? Why was it necessary and how did it enter and affect the human body? How did it change and where? One question led to another all the way from the Dundee sewers to a subsequent life's work on respiration. The next step was a demonstratorship at Oxford where his uncle, Professor John Burden Sanderson, was Waynflete Professor of Physiology, firmly exalting science in a prominently Lit. Hum. atmosphere. The salary of a demonstrator was about £200 a year but there might be pickings in the way of examination fees and so on. It was at this point that John Scott Haldane proposed to my mother, Kathleen Trotter, after a longish period of sitting at her feet and making conversation of a kind which she sometimes found a little uncouth. Yet she had much wanted to be a doctor — about the only respectable profession apart from writing and perhaps painting open to women. Her parents did not allow their only daughter to go on but her interest remained and was certainly partly in the social and public health aspect of medicine and especially in the delicate area of obstetrics.

Meantime the echoes of the old conflict between science and religion continued with many scientists still unwilling to drop the human soul by whatever name they called it out of physiology. My father interpreted all this in his own way. Both my parents would have called themselves agnostics; it was a respectable word. There were times when my father called himself a Christian but usually in deep irritation of official Christianity as expressed by some of its hierarchy. Neither my brother nor I were brought up in any form of normally recognised Christianity but with deeply held humanist ethics, no doubt largely based on the common ground of all great religions.

In science there were vitalists all through the latter part of the nineteenth and early twentieth centuries who still felt there was something beyond what could be expressed scientifically. They were opposed by the hardcore men who asserted that science explains or will explain everything and the human body is merely a piece of advanced technology with some unfortunate mistakes. The "vital principle" was clearly one of those phrases which were used very loosely to mean whatever the speaker or writer wanted it to mean. My father, halfway between, was convinced that he was right. This is something of a Haldane characteristic.

It is difficult to realise now how small the amount of scientific knowledge was in the last years of the nineteenth century and how small for that matter was the number of working scientists in all disciplines compared with today. The British Association could and did invite scientists from all over the world to come to the big annual meetings and these were really forums of science in those days. There was easier understanding between all branches then, just because none of them had gone very deep into complications which might mean a new vocabulary and totally new concepts which had not got through to other branches of science. Consider the number of new words for specific objects or happenings which a biologist, a physiologist, a chemist or even a doctor, above all a physicist, must today carry in his or her mind. No wonder they find one another somewhat unintelligible. Above all they are unintelligible to the ordinary reasonably intelligent person and have the brass to be proud of it!

Some disciplines, for instance genetics, had simply not arrived. Nor were there a quarter as many scientific publications. Many countries such as Japan and India which now contribute largely to scientific thought had not yet started to think in scientific terms, while others like Australia were only just beginning to found universities. My father's colleagues were largely from Denmark and Germany, sometimes France — he always stumbled into German when trying to speak French — and the U.S.A., where he had several friends and correspondents, and very occasionally Italy. He went to stay with the Bohrs in Copenhagen — that is the great Nils Bohr's parents — and there are several letters from their house where he obviously had a very delightful time quite apart from the laboratory work. Once he was there for the Danish Christmas tree where "everyone, including the servants, had to dance round the tree singing a Danish song. Then the presents were distributed. These consisted of all sorts of things — dresses, cloaks, etc. for the daughters and servants and all sorts of toys for the children. The eldest Bohr boy [that would be Nils] got a carpenter's bench. Professor Bohr incautiously lighted his cigar and this set fire to a celluloid top in the end of the pencil. Of course there was rather a blaze as celluloid catches fire very easily. . . ."

At this time the accepted idea of the framework of the human body was only a little more accurate than it had been in Harvey's time. In physiology the functions of the major organs were more or less understood but nobody had much idea of what happened in the pancreas, the pituitary or the adrenals for example.

For my father it was the lungs. Exploring the lungs (which also neighboured the aorta, the heart and the brain) led him from the Dundee sewers into coal mines, tin mines and submarines, up Pike's Peak and down to the sea bottom. Just before he died, when his own lungs failed him, he had been planning a balloon voyage. Always and everywhere he took apparatus which he devised, so that all should be recorded and analysed as befitted a scientist, and acted upon as befitted the kind of man he was.

19

Rick Cluchey

MY YEARS WITH BECKETT

I FIRST began to act in Beckett's plays in 1961 while serving a life sentence at San Quentin in California. Although many other of my fellow convicts had a similar interest as early as 1958, we were all nonetheless required to be patient and wait until the warden of that day decided to allow us the special sanction of an experimental workshop where such plays might be performed. So in 1961, with the advent of our own small theatre, we began to produce a Beckett trilogy: the first works to emerge from this little workshop.

Thus our first effort was *Waiting for Godot*, then *Endgame*, and lastly *Krapp's Last Tape*. In all we gave no less than seven productions of Beckett's circle of plays during a three-year period. All the plays were acted and directed by convicts for a convict audience. And so every weekend at our little theatre in San Quentin it was standing room only for imprisoned Americans; and rightly so, because if, as Beckett has stated, his plays are all closed systems, then so too are prisons. I personally can say that San Quentin is a closed system, a very tightly closed system!

If the critics are right when they proclaim that all of Beckett's characters are drawn from his early life in Dublin, that is, the streets, bogs, ditches, dumps and madhouses, then I can only add that the most informed, knowledgeable and qualified people to portray Beckett's characters would be the inmates of any prison. For here, more than any other place in the world, reside the true Beckett people: the cast-offs and loonies, the poets of the streets, and all of the "bleeding meat" of the entire system. The real folk of our modern wasteland.

And may I say that it was of special interest to us at the time that all over the world audiences were puzzled and fascinated, the critics astounded by the plays of Beckett, while we, the inmates of San Quentin, in fact found the situation normal. Yes, and we did understand about waiting, waiting for nothing. Our affinity with the works of Beckett has perplexed many critics, but never our audiences.

* * *

During my work with the Beckett plays at San Quentin the first rôle was that of Vladimir in *Waiting for Godot*. I was then and am now struck with the simple situation of a man waiting in "fear and trembling"; certainly my own situation at that time in San Quentin prison. Yet too, I was reading Kierkegaard and well knew the old philosopher's idea of a god beyond reason. All I really knew for sure was that "waiting for godot" is like waiting for God. And needless to say in places like San Quentin the possibilities of Him making an appearance seemed highly unlikely. In short, I had no real idea who Godot might really be. However, it was never a problem. I just felt very close to the character of Vladimir, and that too seemed natural and harmonious. Between 1961 and 1963 two productions of *Godot* were given and in both I was to play Vladimir.

Yes, and in my own mind I wondered about the man who could create these plays which seemed so much about my own life. I was being driven mad by my own calendar maker, the warden and the State of California. So of necessity I took up the mask of Beckett's people; Watt and Murphy, Molloy and Malone, the Unnamable. In these works I was to feel secure with the characters, perhaps in many ways because they were so like the people of San Quentin: extensions of dis-connection, decay and uncertainty. "Can it be we are not free? It might be worth looking into." Well, in the end it was Beckett and not the warden who gave me my freedom, a freedom of

21

mind if not of body. Yet the passing of time, the telling of games and of stories was to continue.

In the middle of 1963 I decided to re-stage *Krapp's Last Tape*. I had previously directed a production and one of my associates had directed one; so now I felt compelled to try acting Krapp. It was to be our third production in two years. San Quentin never had it so good, all that stroking of bananas before sex-hungry convicts, a Freudian tease. If Krapp, as I performed him at San Quentin, is a frustrated man, so was every convict in our audience. If Krapp seemed to reject his burden of past misery as being too heavy, so had these poor, bitter convicts. "All the dead voices", a line from *Waiting for Godot*, seems to speak of the situation Krapp is in. He is trying to redeem time, the lost time, his past time; and so were the convicts. Krapp wants to recall a girl in a punt. And the convicts' reality as audience has never been as close to that same desire. The symbols were clear, those bananas, the girl in the punt, the lost time, the light and dark, and the need somehow to relive the past. At San Quentin my Krapp was in a trap, but then so was the audience.

Of course, I never had the slightest notion I would ever meet Samuel Beckett, yet I knew the man or felt that I did. When eventually I was to realise my parole, I decided to come to Europe and quite by chance met Beckett in Paris. It was the beginning of a long and lasting friendship, one which in due course would bring me into greater artistic contact with Beckett the director. The road from San Quentin to Paris was a long hard one for me, but the rewards could not have been more worth while. In December of 1974 the San Quentin Drama Workshop gave a special performance of *Endgame* in Beckett's honour at the American Cultural Centre in Paris. Again quite by chance, I was able to be invited to Berlin to direct a play at the Forum Theatre and, as fate would have it, permitted to work with Beckett at the Schiller Theatre on his own production of *Waiting for Godot* during January, February and the first week of March of 1975.

Beckett, as director, inspires awe. He is so much his own

master, completely in control of his stage, knowing each step of the way exactly where it is he is going. He seems in command of a special art form; one must observe his work with actors in order to realise how simply he unlocks the difficult problems inherent in the staging of his plays.

Theatre legend abounds with warnings to the writer who would attempt the direction of his own plays. Yet with Beckett these admonitions are meaningless. I agree that it is a rare occasion when one finds an author who can place his work before the public in its most dramatic context; Beckett is that man. In the hands of other directors his work appears untidy, flat, too realistic and unpoetic. With actors other problems manifest themselves: perhaps it is mainly the fault of a lack of understanding of Beckett's special form which causes his work in other hands to seem so ponderous upon the stage. Perhaps it has been this lack of understanding more than anything else which seems to have so maligned Beckett's theatre plays. Certainly the critics would agree now that these plays, which in years past have caused much controversy and hard criticism, have appeared more recognisable and fluent to the public. Maybe we had to catch up with Beckett.

I believe Beckett rightly knows his own work and in this he is unique. His Schiller production of *Waiting for Godot* set standards for all other productions, many of which are now being produced in other parts of the world by people who went to Berlin to discover how Beckett would do it. His *Waiting for Godot* succeeded because it was Beckett the artist in full control of the canvas. The shape and style of his *Waiting for Godot*, with its musicality and mime, the beauty of tone and sound, its movement and silent landscape merging, flowing richly and gracefully, was like the form of a fine *mobile* at play in the wind. I know of no other dramatist who could do this with his own work on the stage.

* * *

Following the Schiller production, I went to Paris to observe Beckett's work-in-progress with a young French actor,

Chabert, who was then doing *Krapp's Last Tape*. But after some days in Paris my good fortune ran out and I was forced to return to the U.S.A. I vowed, however, to do the rôle someday again. My chance came with the invitation from the D.A.A.D. to spend one year in Berlin as an artist-in-residence. Some months after my arrival there, Beckett wrote me that he would be in Stuttgart directing his new television plays. I went to Stuttgart and asked him if he might direct me in *Krapp's Last Tape*. He agreed. Rehearsals were then scheduled for late August and I returned to Berlin to await Beckett's arrival.

One of the first things I told myself was that I would forget everything I knew about *Krapp's Last Tape*. I vowed to strip myself of any egoist connection with this work. In a sense I would become faceless, doing only the things Beckett wanted; no experimentation or little actor's tricks. I must become a conduit for the director's intentions, a drawing board for Beckett's design, a stone for his chisel. The rules were simple: I would do exactly what Beckett wanted, nothing more.

At the first rehearsal in his room at the *Akademie der Kunste*, we began working on the tape sections of the play, which were scheduled for recording the following day. We sat for several hours working on the tonal problems: Beckett speaking the text first, then myself. Gradually we both began speaking the text together; the problems of tone and rate, of measuring out the exact space between the words, the sound of those words, the pauses, the silences, gradually dissolved until slowly the whole range of dynamics took shape.

The following day we again sat down and went over the entire text, Beckett speaking the lines along with me, here and there correcting or making a change in the lines. He was very patient when I dropped the tonal or spacial relationships. Late in the morning I finally sat before the microphone in a closed studio, with Beckett outside viewing and listening to the recording. He had a control button by which he could cut in and give me directions instantly. I was very nervous and began to make mistakes immediately. On we went for two hours. We broke for lunch with no usable tape. The rest of the afternoon went the same way. I couldn't get it right. At the end of the first day's recording we still had no usable tape. The next day the studio was not available, so we again worked in his room at the *Akademie*. Slowly during the course of the day I began to catch the tonal variations and rhythm. He repeated over and over again the musical structure of the play, word by word, tone by tone, measure for measure, until the rhythmic whole emerged. And I was to learn that the structure of Beckett's dramatic works for theatre is truly metrical: a coda of unaccented and accented prose, a great measured flow of poetry.

If time is the inner voice of Beckett's theatre, then poetic measure is the sound of that voice from within. A voice full of metaphrase and life, which by some magical composition form a harmonious correlation upon the stage. The second and final day in the studio we pulled it off. Beckett was happy and said the tape was more than acceptable; but if the rest of the rehearsal plan went well and allowed us time, we should return to the studio for one final go at a new tape. In all we had spent four days on the tape section.

Now came the work of Krapp at the table, with his old tins, dictionary, ledger and, naturally, the tape recorder. Beckett demonstrated the precise manner in which he wanted each object handled: every gesture, each attitude, every position of the body; the position in which he broods, the opening position where he is trying to remember. He stressed that everything should be simple, clear and measured. He went over the table attitudes and business with a fine comb, culling the superfluous, reducing every gesture, movement and sound to its exact musical form. He never seemed to tire or become irritated when I failed to get things right. I marvelled at his patience and the economy with which he always arrived at the right point. And as the days passed many of the fears I had about performing a 69-year-old character began to fade. Mainly I believe that as a director Beckett is also a sculptor: he works almost immediately for the shape of his work. It is, by definition, his private world, one in which I became the shape of his idea upon the stage.

Visually the role of Krapp, under Beckett's exacting eye, demanded that I must realise at times a perfect stillness in order to merge with the unchanging constants of light and dark. Only then are the minute, tiny transitions visible. Only with his blend of stillness and contrasting violent sounds does Krapp cut back into the memory of his life. This inner or past life is lost in a sea of recorded tapes, evoking the duality of two lives, therefore this must be very clear in performance.

Beckett directs by inches and seconds, here we find no superfluity of word or movement. Every action is precisely given, riveted to the actor with style and grace, dignity and precision. Each step is counted and every second perfectly timed. Beckett builds repetition upon repetition, silence upon silence. I began in the later rehearsal stages to realise how incredibly full and rich the play had become under his direction and the full impact hit me. If Beckett could build such a functional performance, it meant there would be no escape or exits from these rigid mathematics. They must now be torn out of the actor's soul for every performance, without compromise or short-cutting in the process. The impact hit me: I would now become the curator, the pastor of Krapp's old clothes, his valet and confidant; yet Krapp doesn't have a first name, so what do I call him?

* * *

Endgame, under my direction, was presented by the Workshop in San Quentin in 1962. Here once again I felt on familiar ground. Another closed system, another asylum, another little world wherein each madman becomes locked up in his own mind, a mad game of chess with a mad warden, where each player refuses to engage or move the pieces beyond a certain point. Nagg and Nell in their own special padded cells. Hamm, riveted to his rocker, sits until the end, locked up in his mind. Clov, suffering not really madness, but the utter vacuum of a closed system; cell within cell, in a windowless room within a room. And all of us trying desperately to see over the wall and through the barbed wire. And not even a real dog!

San Quentin prison is endgame lowercase. Uppercase Endgame is something only Beckett could write, while perhaps thinking of a place like San Quentin. Therefore, folded neatly within this equation lies a believable dam of information about pain, reality, and cosmic possibility. As a Beckett apprentice at San Quentin, *Endgame* seemed the proper choice for the director who was just beginning. After all, three of the actors are stationary, fixed to their places by the force of their creator's will; the fourth, a semi-cripple who can move only with the utmost pain and will-power. In 1962 it all seemed so easy, so like San Quentin's grim, daily occupancy of misfits, tyrants, cripples and the lonely, dying, stuffed safely away in coffin-like dustbins.

In *Endgame* a whistle is blown; at San Quentin it blows too, and in both cases, many times for the same reasons. The warden wants something of his several thousand captives, or it is the State's way of telling convicts that it is time to eat, be counted, or sleep, or work. Yet the uppercase Endgame whistle is, like Beckett's vision, something special, a ritual to be sure, but a ritual beyond the mere concerns of daily existence. In Beckett's world, endgame can only be minted in the coin of poetic vision, of future events foretold in protagonistic metaphor, like the sad tipster prophet who walked ghostly steps across the space of time, dumping boxes of darkness on the tundra, sometime after the destruction of that world we all knew. The one nobody ever dared to think would one day be exploded by man's greed and stupidity. The world, our bit of time and space survival-kit. The story of the play about endgame-type survival is here born of visionary gifts and prophecy, a shape of things to come. One might safely look upon *Endgame* as a total view of the void, or, by contrast, a reasonable persona of current events — all of which depends upon your point of view.

Is uppercase Endgame really an authentic echo of future shock? Only time will tell. As one means of traversing the time frame Beckett has laid down, I would like to write about our last experience in a Chicago ghetto, with *Endgame*. The

Workshop production of the play was set on the roof of a seven-storey building and was here staged in honour of America's two-hundredth birthday, in July of 1976. The cast included myself, John Jenkins and R. S. Bailey with Teri Garcia Sura as "Nell". It was the sixth production of the play attempted by the Workshop since 1962, appropriately set in one of the worst slum ghettoes in America. Our audience consisted of residents from the building and some invited guests from outside the uptown slum. Our public sat squat-legged on the warm rooftop, while below, the normal evening's street scene unfolded on schedule. Arson, rape, murder, robbery, burglary, knifings, muggings, vandalism, gang-fights, car-theft and drug dealing were carried out by uptown welfare dependents. A racial mix of ethnic people from poor-whites driven out of Appalachia and other deep south areas, poor blacks, poor latinos, poor orientals, the American Indians and of course the hard core members of Chicago's police department who had to combat the crime and open violence.

The rising sound of police and fire trucks split the night sky, the hurdy-gurdy organ music of a nearby carnival, its double ferris-wheel poking green neon spokes high above ghetto tenant flats, framing endgame against our own performance. Gunshots, fires set by insurance-minded landlords or by vandals weary of living in substandard garbage pits. Breaking whisky bottles and soft guitar music, laughter and screams of hate, the normal blood and sweat of uptown, bicentennial style. And Beckett's play holding forth above these lower depths: the alarm clock and the whistle, the rage and the submission of bent humanity, fingernails dug into the poverty of spirit, holding fast to a dream of something bigger. Uppercase Endgame set like a prophetic halo high above the normal lowercase endgame frozen by Zeno's arrow against space and time.

* * *

Now, as a measure of progress, using *Endgame* by the numbers,

I would like to return to the Workshop's first production of Beckett's play inside San Quentin circa 1962. If the uptown *Endgame* seemed like Omega, the end, then the Quentin Alpha might be considered the chief star, a ray of hope, in our otherwise dismal constellation. Sadly our initial probe into *Endgame*'s active substances was set against another dark sky on the other side of the American countryside. The prison is fixed at land's end, thrust forth on a spiney peninsula estuary, a backwash of the Pacific Ocean, the bog-side of San Francisco Bay. And our stage was the former Gallows room where men and women were hung for crimes against the State between the years 1860-1940. In 1941 California instituted the gas-chamber as the means of legal execution, and this of course left the gallows free for other use. By 1962 it had been transformed into a small experimental theatre by the Workshop. So much for history.

But what of the conditions around the mutant irony of *Endgame*? Given the circumstances of several thousand convicts, locked down in concrete steel-faced coffins; the ominous gas-chamber, twin chairs of death, silent and waiting for the executioner's whistle; the warden's alarm clock and the victim's scream; what of the cruel litany of rejection, denial, pain, loneliness and death? The daily curse from three thousand convicts, echoed by the warden and his guards: *put-up, shut-up and lock-up!* The gang rape, the stabbings, the beatings, the shooting and general holocaust of life at San Quentin. What was the convict reaction to Beckett's favourite play?

Most of the men found it chillingly accurate: but mostly they found humour in this darkest of plays. Perhaps a reflection of the essential human condition, San Quentin style? We must point out, of course, the similarities of certain of the Beckett characters to those of San Quentin's administrative staff, and penal slaves. The warden, Hamm-like in his rage, or by contrast a quiet, cajoling visitor to the condemned cell, offering final life-support and courage to those about to die under the mandate of his signature, legally murdered by the

State. The oldest prisoner, Clov-like in his subservient rôle of come and go, stop, wait, all the while knowing it will never end. The indentured powder-monkey emitting a tiny trail of penal dust as he shuffles through the warden's bag of circus tricks. The Guard Captain, Nagg-like in his dependence on convict help in order to sustain life, in a tomb-ridden job, a dustbin of rules to enforce, all the while dispensing crude jokes about sexual impotence, old tales of good times amid the daily toll of actual suicide, rape and sodomy. And Nell, the truncated, sexless cell mother of every convict's fantasy life: alone, unreachable and somehow masturbatory in her isolation and despair; the bony old ghost of bygone dreams, trapped in steel and painted clown-white, the chalk of death, earth-mother.

So now it is complete and the show must go on. Endgame is really endgame, a parable of upper and lower case. Beckett style.

Don Watson

A HIGHLANDER ON THE AUSTRALIAN FRONTIER

How amiable does the design appear of withdrawing the poor and humble from the miseries incident to their situation, amidst the cold selfishness of an advanced period of society; and transplanting them to a new country where the same odious distractions do not meet them, but where they will all find themselves equal in being dependent only on nature and their own exertions for their support and enjoyment.

—Earl of Selkirk
Observations on the Present State of the Highlands, 1806

How shall we save ourselves after such mercies? What is the Lord doing? What prophecies are now fulfilling? Who is a God like ours? To know His will, to do His will, are both of Him.

—Oliver Cromwell, 1561

The English got the banks; the Scots got the land; the Irish got the pubs.

—Old Australian saying

GIPPSLAND is the south eastern extremity of the Australian mainland. Like so much of the rest of the continent it is subject to droughts, floods and fires on almost cataclysmic scale. But the climate is also benign. Mountains to the north feed rivers which wash vast stretches of pastureland before they spill into the coastal lakes lying serenely at the end of a windswept beach ninety miles long. These days those

31

inhabitants who choose to earn their livelihood in competition with the natural environment raise sheep and cattle; fish for scallops, lobsters, abalone and sharks; or work on the oil rigs offshore in Bass Strait. The others, the vast majority of the population, make a living in the towns — in small businesses, butter factories, on the roads and railways, all of them living off and serving the hinterland and the summer tourists. They elect conservative M.P.s in Gippsland; if they attend church at all it is as likely to be Catholic as Protestant since there have always been plenty of Irish there, and since the last war Italians have joined them; the businessmen join Rotary Clubs and organise things, encourage "pride in the community" and build monuments to their own public-spiritedness; the others play cricket and football and go fishing for mullet and bream in the rivers, or on the sheltered lakes in small boats with outboard motors. It's not paradise but one could do worse than live in Gippsland these days.

It was undeniably a good deal closer to the western conception of paradise in the 30,000 years before 1838 when an Aboriginal population inhabited it exclusively. The Aborigines fished the lakes and estuaries, hunted the marsupials for their flesh and hides, and gathered the fruits the bush offered. They grew no crops, raised no animals (except a dog, the dingo, which ate their refuse and kept them warm), built no permanent dwellings, no houses, churches or prisons, stayed in no place long enough to exhaust its resources. The Aborigines paid no wages, exploited no labour, accumulated no capital. To regenerate its growth and so guarantee their food supply they set fire to the bush from time to time, but in this, as in every other aspect of their existence, they were not just in harmony with the environment but a part of it.

The Aborigines were not of course some inverted version of the hyperboreans. The vagaries of the climate no doubt inflicted dreadful hardships. They practised infanticide, homicide, wife (and prospective wife) beating and, probably, but by no means certainly, cannibalism. It is impossible to resist saying that life in Gippsland's state of nature could be nasty, brutish and short. But not so short as it became after the arrival of the Europeans.

Although it had been seen from the sea for years, Gippsland was not settled until the first Europeans chased their pastoral interests over the Australian Alps to the north. The first of them arrived in the 1830s; precisely when is not clear because they were not anxious to tell potential competitors about the land they had found. In Gippsland, as in most other places on the Australian frontier, exploration was the direct result of the need and greed of squatters — those who began illegally grazing their sheep on the outskirts of the settlement and ultimately won both title to the land and a preponderance of political power. Between the time of occupation and the granting of tenure to the squatters the conflict between the whites and the Aborigines was a brutally one-sided one in which the Aborigines, with no hope of victory, only lost the more by resisting defeat.

Now, while they considered their civilisation to be incomparably superior to the Aborigines', the English demanded of the first Governor of Australia that he treat the blacks with "amity and kindness". Governor Arthur Phillip complied by issuing a poster which made it clear to the whites at least, that they would be as readily hanged for shooting a black man as an Aborigine would be for spearing a white. The Aborigines who saw the simple drawings posted around the settlement presumably got the message about English justice, although they may have found it hard to understand how one man could cold-bloodedly hang another. Possibly they were also repelled by the English habit of flogging wrongdoers — in an average year in the convict settlement, 1838, 5,916 strokes of the lash were inflicted on the backs of 18 per cent of the population.

As the frontier expanded in Australia the Aborigines' traditional hunting grounds vanished along with the sacred sites which bound each tribal group to its past and the environment. Tribes which had lived in harmony with each other for thousands of years were now forced to compete for food. As a result, internecine warfare took its toll. But the

Aborigines were neither skilled nor experienced in wars of conquest and a far more destructive factor was the separation from their traditional land and society. The Aborigines were detribalised and in turn demoralised. More than one observer noted that collectively they seemed to have lost their will to live. Contact with the white society had appalling consequences all over the frontier. They were devoured by disease, perhaps most horribly by congenital syphilis. It was estimated in the 1850s that two-thirds of the tribe occupying the area where Melbourne now stands were infected with venereal disease. It is difficult to conceive of the brutality of the Australian frontier. A settler in southern Australia wrote in the 1830s:

> Several of the men on this establishment are now very ill with the Native pox which shows how they Acted with the Blacks. . . . I am told it is no uncommon thing for these rascals to sleep all night with a Lubra and if she poxes him or any other way offends him perhaps Shoot her before 12 the next day.

Alcohol had equally disastrous effects, in fact it was probably the most important catalyst in the catastrophe.

But the devastating effects of culture contact should not be allowed to obscure the less palatable fact that white settlers — decent Christian pioneering folk that they were — frequently indulged in wholesale massacres of Aborigines; usually because they threatened or seemed to threaten their livelihood, but sometimes because the blacks got "cheeky". Or simply for sport. For instance, at Myall Creek in 1838 three men bound together thirty Aboriginal men, women and children, slaughtered them with guns and swords and then burnt the bodies. To the horror of the white community the men were found guilty of murder, having pleaded that they did not know that it was a crime to kill Aborigines any more than it was a crime for a man to shoot his dog. The largest petition in the history of the colony to that stage failed to save them and they were hanged. The Myall Creek affair demonstrated the contempt in which the blacks were held. It also meant that, in future, whites would be much less inclined to boast about their massacres.

It was in the year of the Myall Creek massacre that Gippsland's discoverer arrived in Australia. Angus MacMillan was born at Glenbrittle on the Isle of Skye in 1810, the third son of a sub-factor on Macleod lands. The family was of tenuously independent means and Angus was not the only member of it to seek better fortune in the colonies. However, if Angus's piety can be taken as typical of his kin, the MacMillans had a staunch Calvinist faith to support them in the very worst of times. And the times could hardly have been worse than they were on Skye in 1837.

While it is clear that the old clan system had supported only a spartan existence in the Highlands, the Clearances which followed the rout and defection of the clan chiefs caused misery and chaos on a scale which rivalled the suffering of the Aborigines during the white conquest of Australia. The effects of the Clearances are well known and one example from the *Inverness Courier* of 1838 makes the point. "Bad weather," it was reported from Skye, "had destroyed the peats and, unable to buy coals or wood, they drew lots to see whose hut and cottages should be used for fuel." Angus MacMillan left a society which was chronically incapable of feeding, housing and clothing its members. It was also a society which tortured the soul of its weaker members with Manichean bribes and threats, and their bodies with public hangings and floggings, mutilation, stocks and ducking stools, and gaols. Take three examples from just one issue of the *Inverness Courier*. Elspeth Hayes was to be humiliated and detribalised. She was "ordered to be incarcerated in the tolbooth of Elgin for the space of one year, and to stand in the pillory thereafter with a label upon her breast denoting her to be a Notorious Thief, and at the expiry of her sentence to be banished from Scotland for life". Alexander Gillon's body was never to return to the earth, for "after your execution you shall be hung in chains until the fowls of the air pick the flesh off your body, and your bones bleach and whiten in the winds of Heaven, thereby to afford a constant warning of the fatal consequences which almost always attend the indulgence of passions". Fanny Manson might therefore have been lucky to be sentenced to only one year's gaol for concealing her pregnancy.

And those who did not meet these various fates, those who found redemption in work which was never rewarded with a full stomach, were exploited by their landlords until such time as they became a "clear superfluity", and then they were bodily removed to places such as Australia where their labour was needed.

Angus MacMillan was probably not forced to leave his homeland, but economic circumstances no doubt pushed him to that decision — but once made it rapidly became in his mind a manifestation of God's will. The diary he kept on board the *Minerva* from Greenock to Sydney records his fanatical Calvinism: he ranted at the passengers who danced and sang as the ship left port — they should have been praying. He ranted at the captain who killed a sheep on the Sabbath. Life was a daily prayer to know God's will and to be shielded from calumny — and life was filled with calumny.

It was not surprising then that he passed very quickly through seamy Sydney on his way to the pastoral country. He soon became manager of a station owned by a fellow Skyeman, Lachlan Macalister. This was the hungry age of Australian pastoral capitalism. By the time it was over — which is to say by the time of the 1850s gold rush — up to 200 separate Aboriginal communities had been virtually annihilated and much of the Australian environment had been changed beyond recognition and beyond repair. One of Macalister's more sensitive neighbours described it this way:

> The most stirring sight which the sportsman can witness is the first view of a new pastoral district; and to the lover of the picturesque perhaps this is the most beautiful scene that Australia can afford. . . . Plains and open forest, untrodden by the foot of the white man, and, as far as the eye can reach, covered with grass so luxuriant that it brushes the horseman

in his saddle: flocks of kangaroos quietly grazing as yet untaught to fear the enemy that is invading; the emu playfully crossing and recrossing his route; the quail rising at every step; lagoons literally swarming with wildfowl. . . . Then mark the change that follows upon discovery. Intelligence of the new country reaches the settled districts and countless flocks and herds are poured into the land of promise. . . .

To some the regions bring wealth, while Anglo-Saxon energy at last triumphs over every obstacle. But nature, as if offended, withdraws half her beauty from the land; the pasture gradually loses its freshness; some of the rivers and lakes run low; others become wholly dry. The wild animals, the former peaceful denizens of the soil, are no more to be found, and the explorer, who has gazed on the district in its first luxuriance, has seen it as it never can be seen again.

Fresh from the starvation on Skye and Barra, this was to be Angus MacMillan's experience.

* * *

MacMillan soon learnt from the Aborigines that good land lay on the other side of the Alps and Macalister, whose flocks were in need of new pasture, sent him to find it. By now MacMillan believed that the discovery of the new land was both his God-given mission and his God-given financial opportunity, and he was not daunted by the prospect of finding a route across unknown and extremely rugged terrain which must have taxed his nerve to its limit. No one could question the courage of Angus MacMillan.

The Aborigines had called the land to the south Cabone Benel. MacMillan called it Caledonia Australis. It was, he declared, capable of feeding "all my starving countrymen"; but until they arrived he was determined that he at least would be well fed, and he established five substantial sheep runs.

Once a port had been established and a track across the mountains blazed, the squatters moved in. Amongst them the Scots were legion, particularly men from Skye. The main town was named Bairnsdale by Archibald Macleod of Bernisdale, Skye. Another was called Orbost. The place names are a curious mixture of Aboriginal and Scots. On the track to MacMillan's main run five settlements were named successively Castleburn, Cobannah, Culloden, Briagalong and Boisdale. The first settlement was called Ensay. To the north of it lies Doctor's Flat, after Dr Alexander Arbuckle of North Uist. Not that MacMillan did not pay his dues to England: the two great lakes he named Victoria and Wellington, and the port was called after the ubiquitous Albert.

The one name that did not stick was Caledonia Australis. A self-titled Count Paul Edmund de Strzlecki, a flamboyant Pole with an interest in science rather than sheep, passed through the area shortly after MacMillan and staggered, starving, into civilisation to announce that he had discovered magnificent country which he had named prosaically but shrewdly after the Governor, George Gipps. Strzlecki's appellation stuck and he was made a Fellow of the Royal Geographical Society, while MacMillan chased sheep in his Caledonia Australis and cursed the "foreign impostor".

It was not always sheep which MacMillan chased. There were probably about 3,000 Kurnai Aborigines in Gippsland when the first whites arrived. By the mid-1850s only a few hundred remained, most of them recipients of church and state welfare. The Kurnai had resisted fiercely from the start, attacking both stock and settlers, including MacMillan's. The white "reprisals" were devastating.

Between 1840 and 1850 MacMillan and his countrymen took to the Aborigines with the murderousness of an old Highland regiment. The motives varied. Massacres at the aptly named Boney Point and Butcher's Creek followed Aboriginal attacks on settlers' sheep. In another instance up to 150 Aboriginal men, women and children were driven into a waterhole and slaughtered in retribution for the murder of Lachlan Macalister's nephew. The discovery of Macalister's body had led MacMillan to form a "Highland Brigade" with which he rampaged through the Aboriginal community for months — legend had it that Dr Arbuckle was the Brigade's piper as well as its field-surgeon. In 1846 an observer wrote:

> No wild beast of the forest was ever hunted down with such unsparing perseverance as they are. Men, women and children are shot whenever they can be met with . . . these things are kept very secret . . . some things I have seen that would form as dark a page as ever you read in the book of history.

* * *

Gippsland was distinguished by another grotesquerie — a classic Victorian melodrama with a Gaelic twist. It had been rumoured from the earliest days of settlement that a white woman who had survived a shipwreck off the coast had been captured by the natives and thereafter forced to suffer their beastly ways. No one was more convinced of the woman's existence than Angus MacMillan who claimed that he had found European clothing and a dead white baby in an Aboriginal camp. He also believed — though it is hard to understand how he came to the conclusion — that the lady spoke Gaelic. Here was a terrible combination of Christian self-righteousness, Highland nostalgia and, doubtless, sexual fantasy. In 1846-47 a series of expeditions were mounted in search of the mysterious "White Woman of Gippsland". At the end of it the administrator of the province, who was convinced that the woman was no more than a figurehead from a ship, testified that at least fifty Aborigines had been killed in defence of her honour.

But, colourful as this episode was, it was an exception to the rule of massacre on the Australian frontier. The fundamental conflict everywhere was over land ownership and use. For the whites, greed soon became necessity and necessity, in turn, often became God's will. Christianity rationalised the destruction of Aboriginal society in an age before Social Darwinism. The notion of the Aborigines as a race doomed by evolution was that of a later generation largely innocent of the massacres, random shootings and poisonings their forbears had carried out.* The Social Darwinists at least distinguished the blacks with the terms "race" or "people": for Christians on the frontier they were at best "God's creatures", in the way that sheep and dogs were God's creatures too — except that sheep and dogs were a greater capital asset.

As if to stamp out forever any Rousseauian fallacies a recent writer, drawing on the Aborigines' more bizarre rituals and their practice of birth control through infanticide, commented:

> If the blacks' disregard for human life, repulsive customs, and disconcerting habits could be explained away as ancestral heritages, as no more than what could be expected of a Stone Age people, they were nonetheless revolting and particularly disappointing to those people-lovers who truly believed a childish, feckless, superstitious band of nomads could be transformed into Good-Apprentice, rock-steady, nineteenth-century Christians.

Notwithstanding the fact that some of the habits of the Kurnai were not altogether quaint, the creature which our writer has chosen to describe as Christian seems to have been either a mythical beast or a deceptively dangerous one. If Angus MacMillan was representative, or the Rev. William MacIntyre of Snizort who arrived in the same year, the Highland settlers sought not only the land but to serve the Lord — to raise not only sheep but the "Altar of God", to establish not just Caledonia Australis but Zion. The land and God's will were indissoluble.

In this scheme there was no place for the Aborigines. They offended on a dozen counts. Not only did they steal the Highlanders' sheep but they refused to conform to Christian ideas about how a savage should behave — they were ignoble in their savagery, discerning rather than orgiastic in their cannibalism, calculating even in their infanticide, and stealthy

---

* Although there are no recorded cases in Gippsland, the practice of poisoning Aboriginal food supplies was common on the Australian frontier. The poisons used ranged from strychnine to plaster of paris.

(like the Viet Cong) in their warfare. They did not live as natives ought to live. They appeared incapable of appreciating the pure reason of Calvinism.

By 1885 the remnants of the Kurnai had become dependent on government or Church relief. A couple of hundred had been herded into a mission station where they were taught much the same catechisms that were taught to children on the Isle of Skye. Some of the Aborigines may have found comfort in this. A missionary proudly declared that one of his black flock had said, "I can see Jesus" moments before "his soul departed to the realms of bliss, to be forever with the Lord". But few of them can have comprehended that they were "gaining a victory through the blood of the Lamb" — they had been shot for having that blood on their hands. The Rev. Hagenauer was simply missing the irony when he discussed his triumph in a book enchantingly titled *Black but Comely*: "The grain of mustard seed began to grow, and the eye of faith saw, like the prophet of old, the little cloud arise, which should pour out the Lord's blessing over the poor Aborigines in God's time."

Nor were the Highlanders struck by the irony of their actions. Or, if they were, it did not stop them from destroying with guns and sheep and Calvinism a society that stood in their way merely because their own society had been destroyed in much the same way by the English. The Lord's blessing seemed to be squarely with the whites, so much so that in the 1850s Angus MacMillan, ex-leader of the Highland Brigade, was made "Local Guardian" by the Central Board for the Protection of Aborigines. In this capacity he was responsible for the distribution of supplies to those fortunates who had survived the pillages of the previous decade.

Although he never recognised the fact, Angus MacMillan was well served by history. He could obscure parts of it from the enquiring minds of travellers passing through. In later years he wrote some of it himself. Then, when he was made responsible for the Aborigines' food, the sight of large numbers of natives gathered near his homestead was interpreted as evidence of beneficence. There is a photograph of MacMillan, taken towards the end of the 1850s, which shows him sitting between two Aborigines whose release from prison he secured. No one seems to know just how he managed to get them a pardon, but such actions no doubt earned him the admiration of humanitarians, in addition to those local inhabitants who were grateful to him for the suppression of the Kurnai in the 1840s. The photograph speaks for both sides of Angus MacMillan: the Aborigines' hands are grasped firmly by his; he looks at the camera with an almost insufferable piety; they look helplessly cowed. No doubt to a mid-Victorian audience only the virtue was revealed.

* * *

And so it has remained. These days Gippsland is dotted with roadside cairns to mark the trails MacMillan blazed — his bonneted head embossed beside the words "Angus MacMillan passed this way". An electorate, a college, a mountain, a strait, an annual memorial lecture, a motel or two and other oddments bear his name. He was and is ubiquitous and ineluctable. He is also a major repository of the community's past, not only through the granite symbols, but through potted local histories, local newspapers, the education system and the church. MacMillan has been described to each generation in the same warm terms — "friendly", "public spirited", "deeply religious", "generous". He would have made a fine Rotarian. But in his day it was probably the Caledonian Society MacMillan founded which played the rôle of assigning worth and respectability to citizens.

Now MacMillan had some marvellous qualities. He was an indomitable bush-basher, forever on all-fours penetrating the impenetrable for someone else's benefit; he was a colourful and eccentric Celt and, it seems, generous to a fault. In some ways he was also a tragic figure: he died destitute, having lost everything to bushfires, droughts and bad financial management. He seems to have been changed by his colonial experience, to the extent at least that his housekeeper bore his two children before they were married, and that he left a large unpaid bill at his favourite bar when he died. He was, if nothing else, less puritanical in his colonial maturity. But posterity bestowed only respectability of course: in becoming a symbol of pioneering courage MacMillan also became a paragon of how a civilised person ought to behave. The pity is that in losing the dark side of the man's character we also lost his tragedy.

If there is an historiographical point to all this it is that Australian historians might do well to investigate the social origins of Scottish migrants if they want to understand the origins of Australian social structure and Australian culture; insofar as Scottish migration was an extension of Scotland, Scottish historians might also find the subject salutary. It is not that the Scots were unique in their land hunger — although they were uniquely successful in satisfying it — or in their brutality and hypocrisy. But no other group combined that hunger and brutality so effectively and emerged from it with the definitive respectability of land and Presbyterianism.

Gordon Donaldson

JOHN KNOX:
Victim of Puritan Mythology

JOHN KNOX is commonly believed to have permanently impoverished Scottish culture by the introduction of a joyless ascetism antipathetic to all the arts, and to his influence is attributed all that is bleak in the Scottish scene, from the austerity of the traditional Sunday to the unadorned nakedness of the more old-fashioned presbyterian churches.

That this accusation has never been dispassionately examined is a consequence of the predominant attitudes towards the man and his work. Knox's detractors have in the main been High Episcopalians and Roman Catholics, who, because they were unsympathetic to his theological premises, thought any stick good enough to beat him with and were not prepared to challenge the popular idea of his austerity. On the other hand, Knox's admirers have in the main been themselves ultra-protestants and puritans who thought austerity no bad thing, and considered Knox's alleged share in producing it rather creditable to him. Their attitude is exemplified in the writings of a man like Dr Hay Fleming, a great scholar but himself a member of one of the more extreme presbyterian churches. Hay Fleming once set out to examine critically the familiar story that Calvin, Knox's mentor, had no objection to taking part in a game of bowls on Sunday. After disproving the tale and, as he thought, triumphantly vindicating Calvin, Fleming concluded indignantly, "Thus is history falsified and good men slandered".

There was, it can be readily admitted, a strain of puritanism in Knox. But in it he merely reflected a tendency of the time which extended far beyond those who shared his theological views. An emphasis on strict morality and even on ascetism was shared by men who were in very different ecclesiastical camps. For example, for a sweeping denunciation of dancing as well as of unnecessary drinking, gambling and "over-long sleeping", as well as other incitements to lechery, we turn not to Knox or to any other protestant reformer, but to the Catechism drawn up in 1552 and issued by Archbishop John Hamilton, the last pre-Reformation Scottish primate. Knox, for his part, was much more guarded, at least on the particular issue of dancing, which, he told Queen Mary, he did not "utterly condemn".

Similarly, Knox no doubt disapproved of profanity in language. But in 1551, nine years before he or any other protestant could shape Scottish policy, an Act of Parliament had been passed against profanity, with a carefully graded scale of penalties — swearing by a prelate, an earl or a lord was to cost 1s, by a baron or a beneficed clergyman 4d, by a lesser laird 2d or 1d, while men of no substance were to be put in the stocks.

Equally, a critical attitude to what seems harmless jollification did not originate with Knox. It was not the reformers who first tried to suppress the traditional May day festivities associated with Robin Hood and Little John, but the Roman Catholic administration of the French Queen Regent, Mary of Guise. An Act to this effect was passed in 1555 and it was reaffirmed by Mary Queen of Scots herself in 1562.

Anyone who is disposed to blame John Knox for the stringency of the Scottish licensing laws should go further back still and read an Act of the Scottish Parliament in 1442, ordaining that no man was to be found in taverns after the stroke of nine hours, on pain of imprisonment or a fine of 40s.

The most absurd charge of all against John Knox is that he brought austerity to the Sabbath. The rigours of the Scottish Sabbath — like so much else that is now regarded as traditionally Scottish — can be traced to English influence. It was St. Margaret, the English queen of King Malcolm Canmore in the eleventh century, who insisted that the Sabbath should be a day of complete abstinence from labour. To forbid recreation on Sunday was another matter, but on this, as on dancing, the Catechism of Archbishop Hamilton was as emphatic as any protestant: on Sundays all men and women should avoid "all idleness, vain talking, backbiting, blasphemy of the name of God and contention, and also all occasions of sin as dancing, unnecessary drinking, lecherous songs and touching, whoredom, carding and dicing". Knox and the first reformers were not unduly strict on this issue: taverns could be open and markets could be held on Sundays, except in time of sermon, and weddings, with their accompanying conviviality, took place on Sundays. Knox himself thought Sunday quite a suitable day for a dinner party. It was not until 1579, seven years after Knox's death, that a statute imposed penalties for both working and playing on Sunday.

It is not difficult to see why there was a general trend towards puritanism at the time. The leading characteristic of the later middle ages had been a breakdown of discipline, moral as well as ecclesiastical, and the Renaissance had on the whole contributed to it. All who are familiar with life in Scotland and other countries in the middle of the sixteenth century would hardly deny that a reformation of "life and manners", as it was sometimes expressed, was overdue. Hence both what is commonly called the Reformation and what is commonly called the Counter-Reformation — in other words the protestant reformation and the catholic reformation — were alike apt to be puritanical. It is true, for example, that in Knox's time the town council of Edinburgh issued a proclamation banishing all harlots from the town: but it is equally true that Pius V, a Counter-Reformation pope who died in the same year as John Knox, issued an edict expelling all the prostitutes from Rome unless they would marry or enter a convent for penitents. Neither the Edinburgh decree nor the Roman decree was fully put into effect, but in Rome the pope succeeded in confining the prostitutes to a special quarter, which was walled in and where special sermons were arranged for their regeneration. The same pope was only with difficulty dissuaded from imposing the death penalty for adultery, and he did take steps to punish excessive luxury in dress or in feasting and even the failure of parents to send their children to Sunday School.

Of course it may be argued that the puritanism of the Counter-Reformation was not destructive of culture and that Knox's Reformation was. But even here some correction to the prevalent views is necessary. People go down to the remains of the abbey church of Holyrood, for example, and look at those broken pillars and shattered vaults and say, "Ah, just see what John Knox did!" The fact is that the transepts and choir of Holyrood had been ruinous since they were destroyed by English invaders in 1544, at a time when Knox was still a priest of the Roman Church, and that the nave stood roofed and entire until so late as 1768, when Knox had been nearly two hundred years in his grave. Many Scottish churches were in a deplorable condition as a result of prolonged neglect, as well as of foreign invasion, civil strife and the hazards of fire and storm, and the main task of the reformers was in truth to restore, not to demolish, churches. On the task of restoration of the buildings necessary for their services they expended considerable energy and a fair proportion of their limited funds. It is true that their attitude was in the main utilitarian, but they were not unappreciative of their architectural heritage, for the cathedral of Glasgow was described in 1581 as "ane magnifik work and bigging and ane greit ornament to this realme".

It is true that church interiors were in the main stripped of their traditional ornaments, but much fine decoration in both wood and stone long survived the Reformation, some of it to be destroyed at the command of the covenanters in the 1640s and some of it to fall a victim to "restorers" in the nineteenth century. There are indications, too, that although veneration of the altar had gone there were churches where the communion table was treated with at least decent respect. Nor is it to be forgotten that, while statues of the saints in general

47

disappeared, the post-Reformation age was one in which many Scottish churches were adorned with monuments to the more ˉecent dead, largely in a Renaissance style and some of them ىhowing a very high standard of workmanship.

There was no need for the reformers to erect any new churches, for the country was more than adequately supplied, and architectural genius began to find its outlet elsewhere. Not long after the Reformation, and within a year or two of Knox's death, we begin to find evidence of an architectural revival which took shape in a new attention to residential buildings. These had hitherto, with the exception of two or three royal palaces, been essentially fortified places, castles or tower houses, with a minimum of ornament. The tower-house tradition continued for nearly another century, though becoming increasingly decorated and refined, but alongside it the purely domestic building, with no pretence at fortification, was appearing and finding superb expression in some great mansions, the finest surviving example of which is the Earl's Palace in Kirkwall (c. 1600). The century after Knox's death enriched Scottish architecture far more than the preceding century had done.

So far as other visual arts are concerned, the main outlet of reformed Scotland lay in the mural paintings and painted ceilings of which so many specimens survive from the second half of the sixteenth century and which suggest that Scottish houses were internally a riot of colour. The execution of the work was not always of the highest quality, but the intention to brighten men's daily surroundings is unmistakable. There is little sign here of the dismal austerity commonly attributed to the reformers. And the subjects of the paintings, while they were occasionally scriptural, were often secular and occasionally obscene. This suggests a rather less puritanical atmosphere than that of Counter-Reformation Rome, where the pope insisted on covering up the nakedness of classical and Renaissance art.

On the musical side, much prominence is given to the account by one of Queen Mary's French courtiers of the efforts of the Edinburgh citizens to serenade her on her arrival at Holyrood: he complained that "five or six hundred knaves of the town came under her window, with wretched fiddles and small rebecs and sang psalms so badly and out of tune that nothing could be worse". Perhaps some allowance should be made for the after-effects of an unaccustomed sea-voyage! The truth is that the earliest music of the reformed church was the work of men who had themselves been educated in music before the Reformation, and if it was bad the fault is therefore not to be set down to the reformers. The men who produced the first Scottish settings of the metrical psalms were men like Andrew Kemp, master of the song school of St. Andrews, Andrew Blackhall, a former canon of Holyrood, John Angus, a former monk of Dunfermline, and David Peebles, a former canon of St. Andrews. It appears, too, that if a musical tradition was thus carried on from the unreformed church to the reformed church, the song schools in the burghs, too, were carefully maintained and fostered.

The most severe critics of the reformers have at least given them credit for a zeal for education, but if any thought is given to the content of the education it is apt to be thought of as a soulless grinding at the classics. However, it so happens that we have a detailed account of the education of a Scots boy who was sixteen years old when Knox died and whose school and university days were therefore passed mainly in Knox's lifetime. He was James Melville, who was educated first of all at the local grammar school at Montrose and then at the University of St. Andrews. He tells us that "by our master we were taught to handle the bow for archery, the club for golf, the batons for fencing, also to run, to jump, to swim, to wrestle" and concludes that it was "a happy and golden time". He goes on to say: "I learned my music, wherein I took great delight, from one Alexander Smith . . . who had grown up among the monks in the abbey of St. Andrews. I learned of the gamut and plain-song, and many of the trebles of the Psalms . . . I loved singing and playing on instruments passing well, and would gladly spend time where the exercise thereof was within the college; two or three of our fellow students played very well on the virginals, and another on the lute and githorn. Our regent had also a spinet in his chamber, and learned something, and I after him." There was surely no lack of either joy or culture here.

If the reformers did not destroy music, neither did they set out to destroy drama. Knox himself not only attended a play, or at any rate what we might call rather a pageant, but seems even to have had a hand in its making: in 1571, when Edinburgh was not safe because the castle was held on behalf of the now exiled Queen Mary, Knox was in St. Andrews and attended a wedding at which part of the entertainment was a play in which, "according to Mr Knox's doctrine", the castle of Edinburgh was successfully besieged and the captain hanged. For some years after Knox's death, kirk sessions were still authorising dramatic performances, even on Sundays, and court patronage of the drama openly continued. It was only towards the end of the century, long after Knox had gone, that a sterner line was taken. The General Assembly first of all forbade all plays based on scripture, which struck at the traditional Corpus Christi day pageants, and later it prohibited plays of all kinds on Sundays. As all days except Sundays were working days, and performances by artificial light were impracticable, this amounted to a serious handicap to the drama.

So far as poetry is concerned, the Reformation era saw both the continued appreciation of the older Scottish traditions and the discovery of new methods of expression. The Works of Sir David Lindsay, containing as they do much ribaldry, were printed in 1568, 1571, 1574, 1580 and perhaps in other years. The poems of William Dunbar, which reflect pre-Reformation piety as well as Renaissance satire, are known very largely from the Bannatyne MS. compiled in Knox's lifetime (1568). One printer of Knox's time even inserted a "bawdy song" in his edition of the protestant Psalter, though admittedly he was censured by the General Assembly. Within a generation of Knox's day, a school of Scottish poets had arisen —

Drummond of Hawthornden, William Fowler, Robert Ayton, Sir William Alexander — whose works do not suggest that the scope of Scottish poetry had been curbed by the Reformation.

Often thought of as the sourest and dourest of Scots, Knox was in fact thoroughly anglicised by long residence in England and long association with English protestant exiles on the continent. Had he died before the summer of 1559, he would have been remembered in English, but hardly in Scottish, history, and had Queen Elizabeth been prepared at that point to readmit him to her realm he might well have settled in England and never returned to Scotland at all. With his English associations, he developed English diction and an English accent — a fact which some of his Scottish critics did not allow him to forget. His first wife was English and he sent his sons to England so that they could have the benefit of an English — and Anglican — education. He was perhaps the chief agent in all time in the anglicisation of Scotland, in both its politics and its culture. The reformation to which he contributed did more than anything else to bring about the anglicisation of the Scots language. The Bible, the Psalter, the service-books, the official documents of the reformed church, were all in English. No doubt this was all a great loss to the cultural identity of Scotland, as anyone appreciates who has read some of the vigorous vernacular which had been used in paraphrases of scriptural passages:

> In the tolbooth Pilate enterit it,
> Callit on Christ and speirit gif he war king.

But we have to remember that the choice of the English language by the reformers was to open to Scots, in the next generation, the riches of the Authorised Version, which, if it was a good thing for England, can hardly have been a bad thing for Scotland. Knox's preference for English ways, his admiration for England, are admitted. But the England which he admired was the England in which William Shakespeare was born eight years before Knox's death.

The truth is that Knox was far too human and far too sensible to do a lot of the things attributed to him. Just how human and how sensible he was is illustrated by several episodes in his own career. He had a healthy regard for the safety of his own skin, on the perfectly rational ground that he was more use alive than dead, and had no thirst for martyrdom. He is quite candid about his avoidance of danger. He declined an English bishopric when one was offered to him in the days of the protestant king Edward VI, on the quite specific ground of "the foresight of trouble to come" — a realisation that Edward would be followed by his sister Mary and there would be a Roman Catholic reaction. Knox's prudence at this point enabled him to escape to the continent after Edward's death, when several of the protestant bishops went to the flames. After he returned to Scotland, but before the success of the reformers was assured, he at one point gave his charge at Edinburgh over to John Willock on the ground that Edinburgh was "dangerous". After the murder of Riccio, of which he heartily approved, when it became clear that the murderers were not going to gain political power, he promptly departed for Ayrshire and then went to England, to return only after Mary was out of the way. Again, when Mary's supporters were holding Edinburgh, Knox went off to the safety of St. Andrews.

When the Regent Morton remarked at Knox's graveside, "Here lies one who never feared the face of man", he was wide of the mark, on Knox's own admission. Unless he meant, rather subtly, to put his emphasis on the word "man", because, by a curious twist, it was mainly from women that Knox had run away — from Mary Tudor, from Mary of Guise and from Mary, Queen of Scots.

Tom Nairn

AFTER THE REFERENDUM

W HAT the referendum experience destroyed was not the movement for self-government — as some enemies of nationalism hope — but a number of false and uncertain assumptions clinging to this movement. The loss of such illusions is traumatic, in itself. However, I hope that the national movements in both Wales and Scotland have become strong, resilient and progressive enough in temper to weather the shock. It need not precipitate them into farther flights of sectarian illusion, and could show them firmer ground to stand upon.

On the other side, I will argue that the way in which the referendum was won by the "No" campaign of Wales, and nearly won in Scotland, was itself much more fatal to the United Kingdom state than the advances of Plaid Cymru and the S.N.P. earlier in the 1970s. The electorate of Wales and Scotland was given a curtain-raiser on the British politics of the 1980s and after. Contemporary Unionism pulled itself together at last, and made a determined counter-attack in its true colours, quite unconscious of how these have altered and decayed. Thus what triumphed in the referenda (or at least, what gloated after them) was no longer even faintly recognisable as the ideology of a great state, confident in its future. It was more like the philosophy of a society on the run, already aware of its own decomposition and able to retaliate only with the weapons of moral despair. Its very success, its capacity to spread already-present infection into mass fever, is what should signal something important to everyone in Great Britain.

I

There is no need here to go over once more the recent history of Devolution. In a short-term parliamentary and party-political sense, we all remember whence it came and whither it went. It was an unloved, undersized, consumptive, hypochondriac orphan on whom the whole future of the family had been inexplicably pinned. Once the pathetically tiny coffin is lowered finally into the sod, the only wreath likely to survive the weather long will be the Unionist one, with "Good Riddance" spelt out in indelible ink.

It is more urgent now to look critically at some of the assumptions underlying the exercise — assumptions which, at least to some degree, many nationalists and independent-minded socialists shared for the duration. In this sense, the appropriate headstone inscription might be simply: "Good Men Believed in Him". How could they? Why did they? Will they ever do it again?

Devolution has a longer history than most of us recalled while the Scotland and Wales Acts were being dragged through Parliament. Vernon Bogdanor's book *Devolution*, which appeared on the eve of the referendum, could hardly be a more timely reminder of this history. Over the last decade British arguments about modern nationalism have been punctuated by ritual code-references to "the Irish experience". If Westminster failed to make reasonable concessions to Welsh and Scottish discontent, then these problems would become like Ireland in time, breeding violence, bitterness at endlessly broken promises, and eventual separation.

Mr Bogdanor's study shows us how one-sided this cliché is. There are all sorts of differences between Ireland, Wales and Scotland, of course, and many reasons why Irish nationalism should have been more vehement and irreconcilable. However, there are also powerful elements of continuity running through all three tales. It is not — or not entirely — that the Scottish and Welsh developments may one day turn into repetitions of the Irish experience. The fact is that in certain crucial respects they never had been different from that experience. Nor, as long as the present constitution of the United Kingdom state endures, is there much chance of their becoming different. The recent referendum and its results have merely underlined this long-neglected side of the truth for us.

The state-principle behind devolution has not varied in the slightest. Michael Foot's statements of it echo those of Gladstone. As Mr Bogdanor writes: "Gladstone believed that the supremacy of Parliament offered Britain positive advantages in meeting Irish claims; since, if Westminster's authority could be retained, there would be more effective government than was possible in a state consisting of two-co-ordinate legislatures (like Austria-Hungary). ...." Where a written constitution would merely constrain the process of political evolution, parliamentary supremacy, being in essence a decaffeinated version of the pre-revolutionary monarchy, "is in itself incapable of being surrendered or impaired". The phrase comes, most appropriately, from a reassuring memo sent by Gladstone to Queen Victoria in 1886. We are not yet in possession of the doubtless identical memos despatched by Sir Harold and Mr Callaghan.

Thus, the ghost of absolutism stays with us. Gladstone believed it was (in Bogdanor's words) "an essential pre-condition for a successful plan of Home Rule". Translated out of the metaphysics of British Constitutionalism, this means that the apparent illogicalities or contradictions of any home-rule formula may be safely ignored, since an omnipotent and kindly centre of power will stay intact, and be able to deal with whatever problems arise. To tamper with the ghost itself is unthinkable. It would mean "constraining the process of political evolution" within one of those straitjackets foreigners have such a mysterious taste for. No more flexibility and muddling-through is one of them.

Before Scotland and Wales there was Ireland; before Ireland there was America. Gladstone was — Bogdanor points out — profoundly impressed by Edmund Burke's view of devolution as the proper answer to the grievances of the American colonists. Prompt, generous, effective action would stop the Irish going the way of the Americans. Extending the perspective backwards in this fashion underlines the verdict to which one would be tempted by consideration of the last two centuries alone: "devolution" is not the British state's remedy for any problem of this order, in practice. It is merely a recurring fantasy-solution, to which certain elements in the constitution of the *ancien régime* lend themselves strongly. We have no evidence that the formula can be realised in any kind of fact, except the history of Northern Ireland — a history governed, as everyone knows, precisely by the will of Ulster Protestants to remain inside the United Kingdom and not get out of it. Any state could devolve power to a minority possessed by this brand of self-determination, for it is under these peculiar (as far as I know, unique) conditions that sovereignty *does* cease to pose problems, and pragmatic, flexible-looking considerations are paramount.

Otherwise, British devolution is simply a history of Micawberish proposals. In 1914 and again in 1979, after decades of debate and parliamentary intrigue, the body politic teetered forward to the point of conviction that here indeed, at last, something was about to turn up, if only people would let it take place. The world's journalists crowded eagerly into the manger, notebooks and cameras poised to record the actual instant of the unicorn's birth. *If only* George Cunningham's 40 per cent barrier was (more or less) overcome, Mr Callaghan's government lasted long enough, or Mrs Thatcher read the constitutional runes the same way . . . there the shining little creature would have been, blinking nervously in the TV lights, awaiting its life of flexible self-contradiction.

If only . . . these incantatory terms raise one up to the plane of supposition upon which alone Devolution can exist. Up there on the high plateau of quasi-regal supremacy, amid the eternal snows of Glorious 1688, Parliament can give earnest, minute consideration to the permissible length of unicorn horns and other West Lothian questions. What this reflects is almost religious faith in the state, in a political system so much at one with and so much in charge of society that the latter offers no resistance to its plans. Hence, it can draw up immense blueprints for changes which will leave everything unchanged, national assemblies without sovereignty, crypto-federalist compacts so cryptoid the unitary state gives not an inch to federalism . . . and so on.

Down here, meanwhile, all that really happens is bemused delay. Years slip away, then decades. Royal Commissions, Speakers' Conferences, and All-party Talks succeed one another, bearing intolerable new problems then grave new compromises to the light. What the Queen's Micawbers always really hope is that the problem will go away, sink out of sight in the course of this interminable limbo. "The British system of government," says Bogdanor, "can best be characterised as one of centralisation tempered by kindness." Proper exploration of the semantics of "kindness" would need more time than we have at our disposal here, but part of what it means is, surely, an utterly entrenched constitutional conservatism so secure that it feels instinctively able to negotiate and compromise away almost any difficulty. Its major historical conquests in the area of social struggle, first with the bourgeoisie then with the working class, have created this hubristic confidence. Any conflict can be institutionalised and defused in the same way.

II

All U.K. Devolution scenarios have unfolded along a woodland trail of "If onlys" where the shape of the forest is hidden from view. Over-attention to the scent on the next tree-stump, or the excitement of the next clearing, makes the menacing overall disposition more remote. The merit of the referendum was simply that it gave us a glimpse from higher up.

In this wider perspective — which can be extended both backwards and forward in time — real, malignant, unshakeable opposition to all such schemes is far greater than the quotidian mythology of British parliamentarism would lead one to imagine. It is merely quiescent or inarticulate, most of the time. But it can be rapidly mobilised into a formidable force, whenever required. Which means, whenever any genuinely threatening change looks likely to actually happen as distinct from being chewed over at Westminster or discussed endlessly on *Panorama* or *Weekend World*, the last-minute unexpected character of such reaction should not cause too much surprise. It is partly a function of the way the system normally operates, and a comment on that operation.

I do not mean to imply that there are *no* conditions under which the Lib-Lab side of the regime could manoeuvre through some kind of knock-kneed Devolution arrangement. Simply that such conditions must be very rare indeed. Only an exceptional, rather accidental conjuncture of powerful progressive government in London, a temporarily demoralised status quo, and effective pressure from nationalists is ever likely to push it so far. Could the post-1945 Labour government have got away with it, had it wanted to? Was there a lost, fleeting window of opportunity for the Callaghan government to slip it all through last autumn, during Labour's sudden return to opinion-poll favour?

Once the underlying strength and nature of the Unionist opposition is more accurately estimated, it ceases being worth while to think strategically in those terms. One cannot base oneself upon barely possible accidents, or lucky lapses. Too many of us, perhaps, had a residual Great Briton within us, telling us to wait a little while longer by the gate, like the plaintiff in Kafka's *The Trial*. It is extremely unlikely to swing open. The only realistic-seeming hope of such an epiphany lay in the growing weakness of the United Kingdom state, its loss of imperial pretentions and spirit. The weakness and loss are a fact. But I doubt if we calculated sufficiently, before February this year, what was advancing to take their place.

In a recent interview in *The Guardian* the historian E. H. Carr said that during the whole of the latter part of his very long lifetime Britain has grown more reactionary. Progressive movements and impulses, after their moments of achievement, have been largely suborned into a society whose groundswell lies in the opposite direction. The Labour Party has been turned, slowly but surely, into a main pillar of the regime. One counter-attack after another, in every area of national life, has stifled and neutered the radical spirit. Britain was less troubled by the 1960s mood of renewal than anywhere else in Europe, and now settles more comfortably than anywhere else into the splenetic neo-conservatism of the 1970s.

Thus, decline can be expressed by intensified conservatism, rather than mere nervelessness. When in power the Left will be more nerveless and impotent, as in most of the years between 1964 and the present. However, it is never in *power* at all, in the sense of being able to use office for radical purposes. So the feebleness masks an underlying rightward shift, the pressure of gathering reaction and mass resentment. And it is only a matter of time and opportunity until this pressure finds a way through the resistant crusts of the old system.

The referenda offered a momentary fissure for all this to emerge. Indeed, the simple incompetence of the government in managing the exercise greatly assisted the effect. The absence of adequate resources, poor information, the fiasco over broadcasting facilities, and Labour's determination to show the Assemblies as their very own gift to the people — all these took the operation away from the established parties and turned it over to *ad hoc*, spontaneous campaigns. Nervelessness fostered reaction, with a vengeance. It was the "No" which benefited from having the usual brakes and cautions removed. Suddenly they found themselves able to appeal, with brutal directness, to what they sensed was the dominant itch of public sensibility. The result was the runaway success we witnessed in the last fortnight or so of the struggle. What boiled up into the anti-devolution movement was precisely the style of crass, resentful, frustrated populism tabooed by the

59

usual conventions of U.K. Parliamentary politics. Were the
nationalists to get control via these Assemblies, everything
would be pretty much like now but worse, *a lot worse:* longer
dole-queues, shorter wages, more jobs for the boys, extra
bureaucrats boxing us in, fiddling politicians everywhere.

Speaking as a calloused veteran of declining-Britain
horoscopes, I must confess to surprise at this. The internal dry-
rot of Britishness is in a quite unexpectedly advanced state.
"All the conviction and determination and passion seemed to
be on the 'No' side," said Ferdinand Mount in a celebratory
Spectator article. "Not one single Scottish or Welsh nationalist
would admit that the referendum showed that the feeling of
being *British* went deeper and wider than they realised. . . ."
Let me reassure Mr Mount that a number of Scottish
nationalists do recognise the feeling's vigour and extent. They
do so with redoubled hatred and contempt since the
referendum, and a more than redoubled sense of historical
purpose and justification.

The Unionist case could not have bitten so deep without
having some sort of recognisable truth in it. Although turned
against us in the referendum vote, that truth is more helpful to
us and more damning to Great Britain than other incidents in
the Devolution saga. What is the actual content of the feeling
of being British? On the stark evidence of the Unionist
referendum case itself, boundless self-disgust and utter
political despair. In one of the most incisive comments made
about the results so far, *The Scotsman*'s editorial of the
morning after pointed out how the main achievement of the
"No" campaign ("a strange alliance of big business and
Socialist conservatism") had been simply to "attach to the
Assembly all the sins which the public associate with central
government. . . . Truly were the sins of the father visited upon
the unborn son". There was a virtually total absence from the
campaign of positive praise for the British way. The silence was
more eloquent than anything actually uttered, by either side.

It remained astonishingly difficult to see (or even glimpse)
the great white mansion the devolutionist savages were intent

on blowing up. The reason is simple. It is no longer there. The actual empire has turned into a crumbling ruin whose only active defence is the mobilisation of its own decay. Its core is resentful apathy and a stagnant cynicism which can — as we now see more clearly — be beaten up quite easily into wilful nihilism, under the banner of individual rights and freedoms. "Less government" is not in our present context a slogan of libertarianism: it is the battlecry of the frustrated, increasingly enraged petty-bourgeois, the Thatcherite "little man" or woman ready to hit out against one farther burden or attack on him. The last generation of British government has turned us all into surly, irritated *petit-bourgeois* in this sense. The Scottish and Welsh referenda were unforeseen laboratory experiments in the manipulation of this state of mind, successful beyond the imagination of the reactionaries. It will not be long before the lesson receives wider application.

Is this only a matter of the deeper race-memory left behind by the footprints of Sir Harold Wilson and Selsdon Man? Alas, it is not. Scars only slightly less livid than those of the referendum remind us of the context in which the campaigns were launched. The months of January and February were passed in an avalanche of British pseudo-disaster; canvassers had to pick their way carefully amid mountains of uncollected garbage, their heads ringing with B.B.C. yarns about callous hospital workers, selfish ambulancemen and lorry-drivers with clubs. All this overflowed quite straightforwardly into the referendum. In Wales and Scotland the climate of incipient *Grand Peur* was merely heightened farther, until the "Yes" campaigners found they had to swim with all their might against the torrent to avoid being washed down the sewer completely.

Another conclusion can be suggested from this thought, one which a Scottish nationalist advances with a humour as black as anything from our annals. North Sea oil saved us from absolute catastrophe on March 1st 1979. The February crisis was a phoney one, of course; but only because Scotland's petroleum continued to buoy up the U.K. balance of payments, and maintain the exchange-value of sterling. Otherwise, the scare would certainly have reached the City and our foreign creditors. There would then have been another haemorrhage like 1976-77, and the votes would have been held in an apocalyptic atmosphere, rather than one of standard British sourness and depression. And it would, after all, have been perfectly true to say, as the "No" men would have said, that the Assemblies were 100 per cent irrelevant to an earthquake of those dimensions.

III

I suspect the virtual collapse of the Scottish Devolution plan will bring historical consequences 180 degrees opposed to the Labour Party's hopes. Labour in Scotland never wanted the confounded thing. They were overruled by London and Alex Kitson, in the way so hilariously described by Tam Dalyell in his book, *Devolution: the End of Britain*. Coralled and whipped along the devolutionary path, most of them remained grumblingly hostile, secretly (sometimes quite unsecretly) yearning for a return to the simple old faith. When campaign-time arrived a great number refused to go through the motions. They stayed at home in the spiritual company of George Cunningham and Brian Wilson. Quite a few of them ventured out into the physical company of these gentlemen, on the platforms of the vociferous "Labour Says No" group.

Thus, Labour appeared at best as rather feeble and distinctly thin on the ground. I do not mean, incidentally, that the Labour and other "Yes" campaigners cut a poor figure in public debates with their opponents. Not at all — when directly matched in terms of general rationality and dignity of comportment, they won overwhelmingly (no matter what members of the Oxford Union thought). Unfortunately the vote was not decided on that sort of level at all. And the Labour Party faltered, or just failed, on the only level where it could have fought back — that of door-to-door canvassing and knocking up the voters.

At worst, the Party appeared angrily divided. Division on questions of principle is nothing new and strange for Labour, of course. But there was a new and sinister aspect to this quarrel, which can scarcely have failed to register with the electorate at large. The left-wing anti-devolutionists justified their co-operation with Sproat, Taylor and the others by the standard "bed-fellows" argument. So we were all in glass houses for the duration. While fair enough in the abstract, this protestation failed altogether in the concrete. Given the unexpected force and direction of the whole "No" tide, there was no real "alliance" about it. The socialist contingent rash enough to stick its feet in these waters was snatched up and borne along by them. Eager to defend Britain, they ended up lending flimsy socialist cover to that British reaction and despair I discussed before.

As ever, "class" remained their excuse for the betrayal. Labourism is supposed to represent a class struggle undefiled by national or regional considerations. This notion led them to disregard the blatantly class nature of the specific division aroused in Scotland by the referendum. The bourgeoisie and the landowners were massively in support of "No", and put a good deal of money where their collective voice was. Surveys of business opinion in the *Glasgow Herald* and *Financial Weekly* showed only a few uncertain dissentients and one or two neutrals. Even the Church of Scotland, which has for years passed solemn motions of approval for Home Rule, broke down under pressure from right-wing scaremongers and failed to speak plainly on pre-referendum Sunday. Below these Establishment heights — as we saw — the lower middle class was stampeded into general desertion of the self-government cause. All this amounted to a classical scenario of European class-based reaction at work. Yet many socialists were so blinded by the mythology of "bourgeois nationalism" that they went along with it. Their eyeballs are permanently locked on the distant view of the great white (Socialist) mansion, and simply cannot focus on the imminent, rising wave of a reactionary all-British nationalism.

There is something in this attitude so provincial, so myopic, that I must pause to underline it although it was not crucial to the Scottish referendum. The paradox of a wave of British reactionary sentiment finding its most stalwart exponents on the periphery is only apparent. Metropolitan ideologies, whether of the Left or the Right, nearly always find their most intransigent defenders among those in a more ambiguous and insecure posture. Different impulses converge to ensure this: simple ignorance of the centre, unwillingness to believe that it can be wholly unlike the images transmitted to the provinces, the desire to prove oneself worthy of hospitality in the big house, straightforward love of a chosen career ladder — and so forth. The point is that Scotland (and very likely Wales too) has become so profoundly subjected to this structure of ideas that it is rarely seen for what it is. Rejection of it, unfortunately, has most often assumed the shape of a touchy, crude nationalism incapable of really penetrating and mastering the metropolitan myth-world. This in turn serves to fortify the latter, in one of those vicious circles ideologies function through.

In countries paralysed by provincialdom, servitude is usually stronger than competing official ideologies in the Left-Right spectrum. It unites them in the same way as nationalism can, but more powerfully and subtly. On Wednesday, February 28th, the *Express* published an emblematic picture of the "No" campaign: Teddy Taylor, Robin Cook, the Very Reverend Dr Andrew Herron, and the current Miss Edinburgh, lovely Dorothy Walker. They are standing arms linked in front of the Royal High School, where our Assembly will never sit, while Taylor explains that this body meant "more bureaucrats, more interference in our lives, and more money out of our pockets". A few inches below, in a special niche of his own, the Tribunite M.P. for North Aberdeen, Bob Hughes, is seen giving a socialist polish to the message. "An Assembly is going to hit the Scots where it hurts," he declares, "in their pockets."

When socialists take to this sort of thing there is no point being too polite. Anti-nationalism has blinkered them as much as the most benighted forms of nationalism could, and made them unconscious of who is a running-dog for whom.

In the event, the class alignment I referred to was resoundingly confirmed by the vote. In spite of the potentially lethal combination of Labour apathy and the upswelling stream of reaction, Scotland's sociological and geographical heartland acquitted itself quite well. If we got a simple majority in the conditions described, then we could obtain an over-whelming one when things change for the better. They are unlikely to in fact, in the foreseeable U.K. political future, but this hypothetical certainty has its own weight after March 1st. We are no longer living in the same country, I am heartily glad to say. Our vision of Scotland has altered, and this may be more important than the temporary paralysis of limbs inflicted by the result.

I believe most pro-Assembly voters did feel they were — in the language of the most active, indeed the only active, campaign — saying something like "Yes for Scotland", and not "Yes" for Mr Callaghan and Michael Foot, let alone Bruce Millan and John Smith. There is an appalling simplicity about this, I know. But that is what referenda are like. Labour in Scotland manoeuvred itself into the worst imaginable posture vis-à-vis the hard choice, that of being torn apart by it. It was divided in superficially similar fashion over the European referendum, and the divisions persist; I doubt whether one could say it was "torn apart".

Except for Enoch Powell and a few other premature English nationalists, entry into Europe was not a life and death matter. In Wales, as a consequence of the language situation, I know that part of the country at least has always felt about national survival in that way. But in Scotland it remained exasperatingly obscure just what most people really felt about it — even those professedly most favourable to one or other of the self-government formulae. When it got right down to it, what *was* their instinct in the matter? Well, for the first time ever, the referendum did bring us right down to it, in a way which largely eclipsed the constitutional niceties of the Scotland Act. It brought us down to reality, and up against the enemy. And when this happened, there were people who did feel they could scarcely go on living if the vote went the wrong way.

This is a very intangible type of observation, which I nevertheless feel to be more important than many visible by-products of March 1st. However, there may be one rather amusing phenomenon of the campaign that points at least towards what I am talking about. This is the rhetorical function of fantasy emigration within it. An astounding and evidently growing number of people could only manifest their mounting passion at the prospect of defeat by saying, more or less: "Well, if that's the way it goes, I'm off!" Two striking public examples of this were, on the "No" side, the Conservative Chairman of Grampian Region, Alexander Mutch. He proclaimed himself as ardent a patriot as any Scotsman alive, but he would be with his family on the first train out if nationalism took over. On the other side, Jim Sillars, of the S.L.P., who played a noble and central rôle in "Yes for Scotland", said that if the Scottish people let him down on March the 1st he would leave for good. "Probably to Dublin," he added reflectively to one of the Glasgow *Daily Record*'s reporters. Other destinations I heard mentioned included New Zealand, San Francisco, an as yet unnamed Pacific island, and Kurdistan.

This was all deeply revivifying. The simple polarisation of the referendum dissipated a good deal of Scotch middle-class mist. And it is a matter of fact that fogs of that kind were an especial curse of pre-referendal Scotland. We had lived in Sandy Mutch's windy, sleekit, after-dinner "Patriotism" for a century and a half, to the point of being often uncertain whether any real backbone sustained it. This is — by the way — very likely the same bourgeois concoction which, over the years, has been fed to opinion-poll researchers, and generated the belief that a vast majority of Scots were favourable to

Home Rule. "Do you think Scots should have a greater say in running their own affairs, Mr Mutch?" "Yes, oh yes, after all we've run the British Empire long enough, have we not?" The Scot's sense of having once been a nation-state will rarely allow him to say anything but some kind of "yes" to such questions. Even if what he *thinks* is something like: ". . . provided it doesn't give any power to those dreadful people in Strathclyde".

A great deal of this spineless self-affirmation was blown away in the result. People were made to line up in some sort of vague battle-order, and Scotland was made to see more clearly that the growth of *real* national consciousness is a difficult conflict, a civil war within the nation as much as a struggle between it and the metropolis. What Owen Dudley Edwards always refers to as "the Scottish cringe" led too many of us to feel that a moderate measure of self-rule ought to be handed down to us, for use by the moderate majority in a spirit of general moderation, as a reward for having been the boy scouts of the British Empire. Had an easy majority been gained for these particular proposals, I fear that we would indeed have enjoyed a kind of cringing Home Rule, and settled into it painlessly.

The Scottish National Party finds itself in a uniquely undressed posture after the referendum. It is not merely the trousers that have fallen, there isn't even a shirt to pull down and hide its shame. "It is the S.N.P. of 1979 which lies at the root of the trouble," wrote Neal Ascherson in *The Scotsman* on the morning after. "Great masses of ordinary Scots may one day give their vote to a national party of self-government, but it will have to be a force standing far more boldly for radical democracy and for the interests of the working class." The referendum vote showed (he went on) that "It is among the working people of Scotland that the national movement, to use that good phrase again, is most firmly lodged. Those were the people who looked at the present leadership and political colouring of the national movement and — most by abstaining — said they did not trust it." Alone (or almost alone) among

67

national parties in contemporary Europe, the S.N.P. had prudently refrained from embracing socialism too openly. It had pinned its hope on the Mutches of Scotland, through a nationalism which had tried to be too many things to too many different social strata, too obviously. There used to be heated arguments about whether or not the S.N.P. was a bourgeois-nationalist movement which not infrequently concluded that it was really neither one thing nor another. But perhaps this was the point. That very vaguery and formlessness matched to perfection the inherited curvature of the Scottish bourgeois backbone. And it is this simian cringe which was definitively exposed by the X-ray of the referendal vote.

When, how will the S.N.P. stand up straight? Where will it get a decent new suit of clothes of the sort Neal Ascherson prescribes, with an honest republican cut and a red Clydeside tie? Not without a hard struggle, clearly, one already under way and being pursued with vigour. But I do not want to explore this prospect here and now. I don't see how things can fail to push in that direction, whether by conversion of the whole movement, by splits within it, by forming new loose left-wing alliances or even new parties. On the face of it, the new landscape of politics looks very like that hopefully imagined by the founders of the Scottish Labour Party three years ago. Whether or not that experiment was "premature" (as cautious folk maintained) it was certainly the scene of all sorts of mistakes, and these were related to the absence of sufficient pressure and initiative from below. We were not at that time yet at the watershed, the objective divide which permits effective founding of new movements. Perhaps we now are, and if so time will shortly tell.

IV

If, as I argued earlier, the referenda were partial, unintended breakdowns in the normal conduct of United Kingdom politics, then it follows that all the incipient tendencies were bound to be released, those of the Right as well as those of the Left. When an old bottle is fractured, all the genies escape together. There is a new confrontation of Right and Left, with potentially new rules and a different kind of struggle.

I have referred a number of times to the history, or non-history, of Irish Home Rule. The point of that, in the usual scarecrow use of it, is that devolutionary struggle in Ireland collapsed into violence. Their "life and death struggle" brought a great number of actual, non-metaphorical deaths. It would be hypocritical of me to omit any reference to this sort of possibility in post-referendum scenarios.

It is the case, I think, that to envisage increased "radicalisation" of a national movement has this potential dimension to it also. Nor is it even difficult to see how that dimension could grow. For there is an obviously phoney, perilous type of "radicalism" which *can* be nourished wherever the nice, left-wing variety Neal Ascherson speaks of exists. Again, the two possibilities may be really inseparable. If it is the case that "Devolution" will never bring about a genuine political birth, then one response is bound to be one-sided, obsessional return to the Independence struggle. "Independence or nothing", no more truck with half-measures, more intransigent rejection of parliamentarist illusions — and so on. But this *in itself*, when not clearly tied to and justified by an alteration in the radical content, the social meaning of a national programme or struggle, will inevitably breed a more right-wing climate propitious to violent action.

Not that, in the Scottish case, the existing right wing of the S.N.P. is at all likely to take to playing with gelignite. This is beside the point. They might very well help to form an atmosphere of that sort while continuing sincerely to deplore each incident which flowed from it. Were this to happen, then there might arise a more inflamed situation where nationalism, reacting against the swelling tide of all-British conservative deterioration, itself takes over the virus of despair and hysteria and sinks to the same political level.

Bogdanor notes in his book — and Owen Dudley Edwards has underlined in many of his — how after the 1880s the Irish devolutionary cause was sapped by developments at the centre. The fight for it became ever harder, against "changes in the intellectual climate at the end of the nineteenth century as Gladstonian Imperialism came to be superseded by an Imperialism based upon *Realpolitik* . . .". In our case, Churchillian Imperialism — based on the decline and shrinkage of *Realpolitik* — has been superseded by post-imperial numbness, and now by festering resentment at this incessant failure and retreat. So our fight will become harder too.

To the extent this becomes true, it means that the question of radicalising the Scottish national movement — that "good phrase", but so far mainly a phrase — assumes great urgency, as well as great desirability. For it is only by the utmost radicalisation, on the level of social and cultural content, that we could hope to contain and contest the wrong kind of pseudo-radicalism on the level of "Statehood-or-bust", the replay of 1314, and all those other ghouls which enemies have always insisted were the soul of nationalism.

—March, 1979.

James Young

THE CLANS AND
THE KAILYARD

IN a study of international folklore and folk literature
entitled the *Horn Book*, G. Legman touches the heart of the
present-day Scottish predicament when he argues as follows:

> There operates also, in Scotland (as elsewhere), a most
> important sociological fact, which, though examples of it
> are not difficult to observe, I do not recollect having seen
> formulated in print. And that is the petrifying but protective
> influence of great military defeats. As the Scots themselves
> are the first to recognise, the whole cultural and political life
> of Scotland is still, basically, attuned to no later period than
> the mid- or late-nineteenth century, except in the neo-
> Marxist atmosphere of Glasgow and the industrial area,
> which has entirely jumped the nineteenth century, into the
> present, owing to the challenge of the industrial blight.

Perhaps, then, there is a sense in which the Rebellion of 1745
represented (at least in psychological terms) a "great defeat"
for modern Scotland; for if Bonnie Prince Charlie marched, in
the language of the English socialist historians G. D. H. Cole
and Raymond Postgate, into the "bourgeois society" of
England with "a feudal army", then the Duke of Cumberland
marched into the feudal society of the Highlands with a
bourgeois army. And that army helped to impose capitalism
on Scottish society, with the moral, spiritual and physical
assistance of the makers of the Scottish Enlightenment.

But if present-day Scotland is still stuck in the nineteenth
century the so-called international gathering of the Clans

71

ought to force Scots to ask themselves at least two questions. Will the recent gathering of the Clans in Edinburgh help to reverse or to reinforce this tendency? Will it assist or hinder those modern Scots who are struggling to rescue the country from the myths and mythology about the past? If the answer to these questions is not already obvious, John Prebble's intervention in the controversy provides us with a few pointers. For Prebble's contribution to the debate so far can only serve to perpetuate the whole Kailyard myth.

A recent debate in *The Scotsman* on the nature and significance of Highland Clearances revealed incredible ignorance of the facts of modern Scottish history; and the Scottish universities must accept a considerable degree of responsibility for this appalling situation. Indeed, the Scottish universities have not encouraged a debate on the national question, or the predicament of the "inarticulate Scot", or even on the rôle of the universities in Scotland moving towards self-government; and they have done precious little to encourage a critical examination of the relevance of the international gathering of the Clans in a society still suffering from emigration, insecurity, mass unemployment and urban deprivation. By their apathy, if not indifference, they have helped to reinforce the Kailyard mythology of which the so-called international gathering of the Clans is the latest expression; and the upshot is that instead of producing Scottish E. P. Thompsons, we depend on outsiders to interpret our history for us.

Far from helping contemporary Scots to understand the nature of the Highland Clearances in the context of an evolving free-enterprise economic system, John Prebble simply creates the new myths that continue to distort our understanding of modern Scottish society. This is not to deny that he has done useful work, and it is certainly not to withdraw fraternal support when he incurs the wrath of the Anglo-Scottish landed aristocracy including the Duchess of Sutherland. But the nature of Prebble's analysis compels him to criticise the international gathering of the Clans; but he does not do so for the same reasons as socialists or, if I dare use the phrase, progressive nationalists. For in answer to his own question, where are the Highlanders? he produces a one-word answer, "gone".

In his book, *The Highland Clearances*, Prebble's answer to the question, "Where are the Highlanders?" is clear-cut: "The people did not return to the Highlands. When Australian mutton and Australian wool, bred and sheared by the children of the emigrants, destroyed the wealth of the True Mountain sheep, the land was given to the deer and the sporting rifle." And again: "The lowlander has inherited the hills, and the tartan is a shroud." As well as exaggerating the conflict between Gael and Gall, between Highlander and Lowlander, as well as providing an implicit rationale for the Union of 1707, this sort of analysis distorts what really happened in Scotland historically.

Now, contrary to Prebble, the really important Highland clansmen (that is, important in terms of our understanding of Scottish history and the continuing predicament of "inarticulate Scots" in search of their national identity) did not go to Canada, America or Australia: they went into the cotton mills, coal mines and, later on, the factories and shipyards of Clydeside.

Alexander Robertson and Alexander MacDonald, the Scottish miners' leader who claimed to be descended from Bonnie Prince Charlie, played a major rôle in unifying Highlanders, Lowlanders and Irish immigrant industrial workers; and evidence of their presence in Scottish history will not be found in the Clan Museums in the Highlands today.

In the Clan Robertson Museum, at the Falls of Bruar, Perthshire, there is a photograph of Alexander Robertson, the Chief of Clan "Dundonnachie", in Highland dress; but the curator and the members of the Clan who administer the museum know practically nothing of his important rôle in Scottish history; and even if they did, they would not be able to accommodate him within a meaningful analysis of the rôle of the Highland clans in modern Scottish history. In so far as the

Clan Museums embody any historical awareness at all, it is a false awareness that was sent back to the Highlands in the late nineteenth and early twentieth centuries by an exiled Highland élite who fulfilled the sociological rôle of a sort of cultural Charity Organisation Society.

In the 1850s Alexander Robertson contented himself with writing books and pamphlets on Scottish problems, and particularly pamphlets dealing with the on-going Clearances; but by 1868 this quiet, studious intellectual was leading Highlanders in Dunkeld into "direct action" against the landed aristocracy, that is Highlander against Highlander or the Highland-Scot against the Anglo-Scottish exploiter.

In 1868 the Chief of "Dundonnachie" decided to challenge the Duke of Atholl for taking toll money from Free Church members who used his bridge in Dunkeld; and he was supported by the whole of the Scottish labour movement. The *Glasgow Sentinel*, the main Scottish working-class newspaper, supported Robertson's "direct action" methods of struggle in an editorial entitled "How Highlanders Abolish Tolls: the Revolt of a Clan". Though troops were called in after Robertson organised several physical attacks on the Duke's bridge, the Clan's agitation was successful. Indeed, Robertson considered standing as "a Working Man's Candidate" in the city of Perth in 1878; and in that same year the Roads and Bridges Act abolishing tolls was pushed through Parliament. But the vicious, witch-hunting Scottish Establishment had old scores to settle with the Chief of "Dundonnachie"; and the winners who usually write history portrayed him as a mad eccentric and threw him into a lunatic asylum. Just as they previously depicted John Duncan, the Dundee Chartist, as a "lunatic", and they subsequently dubbed John MacLean a "lunatic", so they resolved the dilemma of integrating Alexander Robertson into the Scottish story by declaring him mentally unsettled. His last pamphlet, written in 1884, *Hanged for the Game Laws*, was a defence of two miner-poachers who, in self-defence, shot and killed two of Lord Rosebery's game-keepers.

The oral evidence of Bob Selkirk, a veteran Scottish socialist who died in 1974, demonstrates that the primitive egalitarian social values of the Highlanders who ended up as coal miners in the West of Scotland did not die as Highland peasants were gradually turned into modern proletarians. In a pamphlet published in 1867 entitled *Our Deer Forests*, Alexander Robertson defended poachers and poaching, since game and the birds of the air belonged to everyone rather than a small élite of landed aristocrats. And though Bob Selkirk did not know anything of Alexander Robertson either, he recalled that the two miners whom "Dundonnachie" had defended in *Hanged for the Game Laws* were heroes in the mining communities. As Bob Selkirk explained in a letter to me before his death: "Poaching was not regarded as a crime. When a child I often heard remarks which seemed to imply that a man who was hanged for shooting a gamekeeper was a hero. I think his name was McVickers and the gamekeeper was shot somewhere in the Rosewell area of Midlothian. Poaching was widespread, the idea which dominated the thinking was that 'the Laird had no right to the game' and 'we are not going to starve'."

But there are other problems inherent in Prebble's analysis of the Highland Clearances; for it is not just that he ignores the Highlanders who ended up in the coalfields of the West of Scotland. It is not just that "kinship" or "blood ties" in a complex, modern industrial society is romantic nonsense. It goes much deeper than that; for like the Highland chiefs of legend and myth whom he criticises so well, he thinks that the Clearances were inevitable. And the problem for liberals as well as socialists is this: how do you criticise morally an inevitable historical process?

This problem is at the heart of much contemporary Scottish confusion over the national question, of the search of Scots for a meaningful sense of national identity; and the old Frederick Engels (as distinct from the young Marx) does not help to resolve the dilemma. In a letter that the old Engels sent to Bernstein, the German socialist revisionist, in 1883, Engels justified the Highland Clearances. He confessed himself sufficient of an authoritarian to view the presence of such people "in the midst of Europe" as "an anachronism"; and it is this kind of authoritarianism and sometimes mindlessness that Scottish socialism has been particularly prone to succumb to. But that is not the real problem for either historians or socialists or progressive nationalists; the point is that history is made by people, unless one is a determinist in the Presbyterian or in the Stalinist mould.

And once again we touch on the central weakness of Prebble's analysis; the assumption that the rank-and-file Highlanders were *totally helpless* victims of history, like the Jews in Nazi Germany, caught in the grip of impersonal social, economic and political forces beyond their ken. It is not just that he sees them as victims during the main period of the Clearances; but that even in the 1880s what he calls "the cause of the (Highland) people" was taken into Scottish politics by outside Highland forces, the Land Restoration League. This was not so. Indeed, the issue of the Clearances was raised in Scottish society in the 1880s by the children, grandchildren and great-grandchildren of the dispossessed Highlanders. In the Highlands, in the trades councils, sometimes in the Free Church, in the Scottish Land and Labour League and in the Scottish Liberal Association, the Clearances became a source of polemic and debate. Moreover, it was the working-class radicals, some of whom were literally as well as metaphorically the children of the dispossessed clansmen, who pushed the Scottish Liberal Association into supporting the campaign against the landed aristocracy in Scottish society as a whole, Scottish Home Rule, the legal eight-hour day and land nationalisation.

In contrast to some latter-day, would-be socialists they did not assume that the Union of 1707 was the beginning of Scotland's evolution in the direction of modernisation and civilisation; they did not believe in the glorification of the proletarian status *per se* or the cult of the proletarian he-man; and they did not think that industrialisation was innately and unquestionably progressive. They subscribed to the socialist dream; but they did not think it was automatically incompatible with the preservation of minority cultures or Scottish self-government.

Since then the works of the great socialist thinkers have become far more widely available and the twin experiences of Stalinism and fascism have helped to discredit the socialist dream. Totalitarianism threatens us all: the ever-present threat of what socialists in the early part of the century called the "Servile State". But part of the problem of socialism in Scotland — the problem of how we evaluate the significance of the international Gathering of the Clans — is simply one of rediscovering our own history and of integrating the problem of "modernisation" and Clearance, whether of Highland clansmen after 1745 or Clydeside shipyard workers in 1971, into an intelligent, humane and compassionate, socialist analysis of the problems facing modern Scotland.

This problem is not just relevant to the future of contemporary Scotland: it also touches the core of the dilemma of modern socialism. In recent months I have heard socialists condemn the 7:84 Theatre Company for blurring the socialist message by concentrating on the national question — the same socialists who unashamedly defend the Highland Clearances in the name of "modernisation", "progress" and "inevitability". As Raymond Williams puts the same point:

> The great indictments of capitalism, and of its long record of misery in factories and towns, have co-existed, within a certain historical scheme, with the repeated use of "progressive" as a willing adjective about the same events. We hear again and again this brisk, impatient and as it is said realistic response: to the productive efficiency, the newly liberated forces, of the capitalist breakthrough . . . as if the exploitation of resources could be separated from the exploitation of men.

It is this kind of abstractionism — the abstractionism Williams criticises — that vitiates the socialist dream; that prevents working men and women and middle-class men and women from moving into action to translate the dream into a reality; and it is the same abstractionism that has led to the intellectual degeneration of the Scottish labour movement and its lack of sympathy with the aspirations of the many Scots who now want some form of self-government. Moreover, it is at the root of the failure to understand the real significance of the international gathering of the Clans from a socialist standpoint: a failure of the socialist critique which makes it possible for such a ridiculous thing as this gathering to obscure the facts of actual Scottish history.

Neal Ascherson

LIFE WITH THE HEIGHOS

THINK of a great, sere countryside. Scattered over its surface, there lives a peasantry divided into two races. There are those — the mass of them — who inhabit ordinary cottages and bothies, managing adequately in good seasons but at the mercy of the drought. There are, however, others who stay in stone houses passed on from generation to generation, living sometimes austerely but after good rains with a mysterious ease and opulence.

This is on its surface a dry country. The mass live on land irrigated only by rainfall. Here and there, the air traveller sees the twinkle of dams, some built by the state in recent years and many more by private people, which mitigate times of drought and pass on stored-up rainwater — often at a price — to the ordinary peasants. But deep under that surface there lies a subterranean lake, a buried water-table.

And the stone-housed people have wells. This is their secret. In the yards of their farms stand old Victorian headworks of iron, covering the shaft which reaches down through the beds of light soil and clay to the geological depth where the water lies. It is not the most modern equipment, only a trickle of water reaches the surface, enough to keep a few beasts alive and to irrigate the vegetable garden but still more than anything which can reach the rain-dependent majority. When times improve, though, and long rains or heavy winter snow have raised the water-table closer to the surface, the crops around the house grow with a richness and variety which the rain people cannot achieve.

This is a simile for traditional English middle-class wealth. The rain people are wage-earners, directly subject to the fluctuations of employment, inflation, pay-packets. The dams are the accumulations of wealth which are immediately visible on the surface of society: the fortunes of the speculators and the resources of the Welfare State. And the stone-house dwellers are those, whether they are themselves active capitalists or in the salariat or merely rentiers and maiden aunts or even well-spoken tinkers flogging cheesecloth blouses down the Portobello Road, who have access to the accumulated wealth of the ancient English middle-class.

"Access" is the important word. It isn't so much a matter of outright possession. We know that England is still a country of spectacular inequality in the matter of actual ownership of money and property, so far as this heavily private matter can be discovered and measured. While 90 per cent of the land in England and Wales was still tenanted (i.e. in estates) in 1880, no less than 50 per cent was still tenanted in 1975. Estimates of total wealth held by percentages of the population swing about a good deal (the "7:84" formula is one of many), with J. R. Revell calculating that the top 5 per cent in Britain as a whole owned 75 per cent of the wealth in 1960, and the Open University's "Patterns of Equality" course suggesting that the top 25 per cent own 70 per cent of wealth. But beyond this lies the question of who — beyond the titular possessor — has a standard of living or way of life which is dependent upon that money.

How does the old British elite so serenely survive? How — to put it another way — is it possible for a married couple aged about thirty-five and earning, say, £5,000 a year* to own a house in Islington or Chelsea worth £35,000 and send two children to private schools charging at least £1,000 a year? In some ways, it is better to go back a few years, before the explosion in London house prices, and to ask how in 1960 a

---

* This article was written in 1970. Such male salaries have since risen enormously in relation to property values, etc.

young married man earning £1,500 could set about buying a
house which then cost £7,000-£8,000?

* * *

To call upon Charles and Melissa Heigho wouldn't have
told you much. Rush matting, a few nice rugs, one or two small
but very good bits of antique furniture, a "daily woman", quite
likely no car "because we can't afford one". Television by
Radio Rentals, underpants by Marks and Sparks. "Wealthy"
is obviously the wrong word. Inspecting Charles's bank
account would probably show a small but painful overdraft,
no more than a hundred quid or so but the subject of much
remonstration at home, and possibly a few hundred in a
deposit account or building society.

Yet this is where the English ruling class is reproducing
itself, discreetly ensuring another generation of security and
privilege within the Secret Garden whose key no fumbling
socialist Chancellor has yet discovered. The bulge under
Melissa's gingham smock is another little Public Schoolboy,
destined for the administrative grade of the Civil Service, a
place in a merchant bank or a Headship of Chancery in some
embassy. And he too will grow up without much cash but with
things which only substantial money can buy: more of them if
capitalism is thriving and fewer if there is a season of social-
democrat austerity.

We all know that the age of the mighty private entrepreneur
is gone. Charles's grandfather built railways in South America,
beating down Indian insurrections with a golf club. His great-
uncle patented a new chemical bleach and poured sulphurous
torrents of waste into Yorkshire rivers. Melissa's great-
grandfather was a Cornish tin-miner who rose to marshal
diamond-mining Kaffirs in Griqualand West. All that is over.
Nobody in either family, it's probable, is creating wealth in
that way now. The male descendants earn salaries, good or less
good, with a larger farmer here or there and perhaps the odd
owner of an advertising agency. What we are dealing with is

the most discreet, sophisticated and effective system of wealth *transmission* the world has ever seen.

The fortunes of the *Grüderzeit* have gone into family trusts. Capital is invested in stocks and shares. Often a part of this investment remains in the shares of private companies, that secret and unquantified sector of British capitalism whose shares have only a nominal value in public but which represent infinitely higher sums if they should ever be realised.

As far as possible, this capital must remain intact and undistributed. Primogeniture helps here. When Charles's father dies, he will leave his share of old "Venezuela" Heigho's money in a will-trust, the income of the investments to support his widow while she lives, and his children will receive only token sums at his death. When Charles's mother dies, the capital may be subdivided among the children but most of it will probably stay with the eldest son who may decide to spend some of it — against the frantic advice of family lawyers and the bitter opposition of his relations — but is expected to transmit the main capital once more through his own will-trust. He does not have to do so: English law permits him to leave his money to a cats' home, especially if he has no children, or to the Symbionese Liberation Front. But convention usually wins.

Three particular features of English middle-class *mores* arise from this. The first is the common spectacle of relative austerity in the midst of unrealised wealth. The income from shares in such a trust may often be quite small, and in the case of private family companies, exiguous. Outside conditions matter too. In the post-war period, very little water was reaching the surface: income from shares was slight, the trappings of wealth were scarce and extremely costly, and the possibility of actually making money through buying and selling — the sale of houses or land, for instance — was bleak. In these circumstances, with the water-table intact but exceptionally difficult to bring up to ground-level where it could be used, the English upper classes presented a picture of impressive dilapidation. "Poor as church mice," they used to say, "the Brondesburys are eating cold rice pud off gold plates."

Matters had become very different by the mid-sixties. Americans who had sent the Brondesburys CARE Parcels and Hershey bars in return for a look at the Muniments Room now scratched their heads: how could the church mice be driving two new cars, paying Eton fees and flying to Rhodesia for Christmas? The answer lay of course in the revival of share income and the lavish possibility of capital gains. To borrow from a family trust against prospects, a request once rejected with outrage by trustees and solicitors, was now frequently tolerated.

The young must still, in general, do without "their" money. But even in the worst times, the spirit of the trust is respected: a certain standard of living is essential. Somehow the odd few thousand to put down on a house is almost always forthcoming, the trust offering large sums at very low rates of interest on security of the house itself — no bad deal for posterity, as it turned out. A third of the price of Charles's first house will have been provided in this way, possibly more, although he must raise a mortgage to provide for the balance.

The second feature is the arrant sexism of the system. This isn't merely the habit of primogeniture in favour of sons. It is the moral pressure laid upon widows, whose survival — often on an income stingy in proportion to the capital involved — denies "my money" to impatient children and beneficiaries. Alienated money becomes a monstrous fetish impossible to propitiate: the woman who persuades the trustees to disgorge in favour of her children is betraying the Mosaic law of English class maintenance, while by refusing to permit a distribution she may make her children wish her dead. Literature has spread the notion that old women "enjoy" power of this kind, one of the crueller sexist myths.

And thirdly, there is the importance of death, the Spring Festival of rentier capitalism. Birth is an event of slight importance, save for the clan's responsibility to take out insurance policies guaranteeing the boy's fees at a public school. Marriage matters little more, especially now that the "marriage settlement" (that tribal arrangement which created a new trust whose income was to supply the young couple, but which would be broken up if the marriage were dissolved) has become so rare. Death, however, brings about the creation of new trusts, the distribution of money, the casting-off of old investment patterns and older family advisers. In the office of the Heighos' solicitors, one more black tin box stuffed with papers is added to the stack, the name of the corpse painted carefully in white on the side. Another will drags towards probate: another baby trust is born.

Abstinence, fear of women, the celebration of death. No wonder the English middle class took over the Druid legends as their myth or origin. The transmission of wealth, so beautifully articulated to the maintenance of domination in the professional and state élites, remains proof against almost any disaster save social revolution or a sustained hyper-inflation. But the kindness and tolerance of the English middle class (rather less impressive than the kindness and tolerance they have contrived to mediate to the English masses who put up with them still) is born of the confidence of an Order, a melancholy Druidic caste, and not from a sense of individual vigour. Just as their huge reservoir of wealth is used largely to maintain social identity rather than to generate production, so well-born English businessmen will convey that they make money out of reluctant duty rather than because they want to be rich.

The great eighteenth-century antiquary William Stukeley got it right in his poem "The Druid":

> *From grinding care and thrift secure,*
> *Arrived at years of life mature,*
> *Unenvy'd for a Fortune great;*
> *Above contempt for low estate,*
> *Let the remainder of my days*
> *In private life serenely pass.*
> *Unnotic'd I would chuse to dwell,*
> *Yet in a house, and not a Cell. . . .*

James Baldwin

OF THE SORROW SONGS:
The Cross of Redemption

July 29, 1979

I WILL let the date stand: but it is a false date. My typewriter has been silent since the 6th of July, and the piece of paper I placed in the typewriter on that day has been blank until this hour.

The 29th of July was — is — my baby sister's birthday. She is now thirty-six years old, is married to a beautiful cat, and they have a small son, my nephew, one of my many nephews. My baby sister was born on the day our father died: and I could not but wonder what she, or our father, or her son, my nephew, could possibly make of this compelling investigation* of our lives.

It is compelling indeed, like the nightmare called history: and compelling because the author is as precise as he is deluded.

Allow me, for example, to paraphrase, and parody, one of his statements, and I am not trying to be unkind:

> There have been two authentic geniuses in jazz. One of them, of course, was Louis Armstrong, the much loved entertainer, striving for acceptance. The other was a sociopath named Charlie Parker, who managed . . . to destroy his career — and finally himself.

* *The Making of Jazz* by James Lincoln Collier (New York, 1979).

85

Well. Then: *There have been two authentic geniuses in art. One of them, of course, was Michelangelo, the much beloved court jester, striving to please the Pope. The other was a misfit named Rembrandt, who managed . . . to destroy his career – and finally himself.*

If one can believe the first statement, there is absolutely no reason to doubt the second. Which may be why no one appears to learn anything from history — I am beginning to suspect that no one *can* learn anything from the nightmare called history — these are my reasons, anyway, for attempting to report on this report from such a dangerous point of view.

I have learned a great deal from traversing, struggling with, this book. It is my life, my history, which is being examined — defined: therefore, it is my obligation to attempt to clarify the record. I do not want my nephew — or, for that matter, my Swiss godson, or my Italian godson — to believe this "comprehensive" history.

People cannot be studied from a distance. It is perfectly possible that we cannot be studied at all: God's anguish, perhaps, upon being confronted with His creation. People certainly cannot be studied from a safe distance, or from the distance which we call safety. No one is, or can be, the other: there is nothing in the other, from the depths to the heights, which is not to be found in me. Of course, it can be said that, "objectively" speaking, I do not have the temperament of an Idi Amin, or Somoza, or Hitler, or Bokassa. Our careers do not resemble each other, and, for that, I do thank God. Yet, I am aware that, at some point in time and space, our aspirations may have been very similar, or had we met, at some point in time and space — at school, say, or looking for work, or at the corner bar — we might have had every reason to think so. They are men, after all, like me; mortal, like me; and all men reflect, are mirrors for, each other. It is the most fatal of all delusions, I think, not to know this: and the root of cowardice.

For, neither I, nor anyone else, could have known, from the beginning, what roads we would travel, what choices we would make, nor what the result of these choices would be: in ourselves, in time, and space, and in that nightmare we call history. Where, then, is placed the "objective" speaker, who can speak only after, and never before, the fact? Who may, or may not have perceived (or received) the truth, whatever the *truth* may be? What does it mean to be *objective*? what is meant by *temperament*? and how does temperament relate to experience? For I do not know, will never know, and neither will you, whether it is my experience which is responsible for my temperament, or my temperament which must be taken to task for my experience.

I am attacking, of course, the basis of the language — or, perhaps, the *intention* of the language — in which history is written — am speaking as the son of the Preacher-Man. This is exactly how the music called *jazz* began, and out of the same necessity: not only to redeem a history unwritten and despised, but to checkmate the European notion of the world. For, until this hour, when we speak of history, we are speaking only of how Europe saw — and sees — the world.

But there is a very great deal in the world which Europe does not, or cannot, see: in the very same way that the European musical scale cannot transcribe — cannot write down, does not understand — the notes, or the price, of this music.

Now, the author's research is meticulous. Collier has had to "hang" in many places — has "been there", as someone pre-dating *jazz* might put it: but he has not, as one of my more relentless sisters might put it, "been there and back".

My more relentless sister is, merely, in actuality, paraphrasing, or bearing witness to, Bessie Smith: *picked up my bag, baby, and I tried it again.* And so is Billie Holiday, proclaiming — not complaining — that *my man wouldn't want me no breakfast/wouldn't give me no dinner/squawked about my supper/and threw me out doors/had the nerve to lay/a matchbox on my clothes.*

I didn't, Billie tells us, *have so many. But I had a long, long ways to go.*

Thus, Aretha Franklin demands *respect*: having "stolen" the song from Otis Redding. (As Otis Redding tells it: sounding

strangely delighted to declare himself the victim of this socio-
pathological act.) Aretha dared to "steal" the song from Otis
because not many men, of any colour, are able to make the
enormous confession, the tremendous recognition, contained
in *try a little tenderness.*

And: if you can't get no satisfaction you may find yourself
boiling a bitch's brew while waiting for someone to bring me
my gin! or start walking toward the weeping willow tree or
ramble where you find strange fruit — black, beige, and brown
— hanging just across the tracks where it's tight like that and
you do not let the sun catch you crying. It is always: *farewell to
storyville.*

For this celebrated number has only the most passing, and,
in truth, impertinent, reference to the red-light district of New
Orleans, or to the politician for whom it was named: a certain
Joseph Story. What a curious way to enter, briefly, history,
only to be utterly obliterated by it: which is exactly what is
happening to Henry Kissinger. If you think I am leaping, you
are entirely right. Go back to Miles, Max, Dizzy, Yard-Bird,
Billie, Coltrane: who were not, as the striking — not to say
quaint — European phrase would have it, *improvising*: who
can afford to improvise, at those prices?

By the time of *Farewell to Storyville*, and long before that
time, the demolition of black quarters — for that is what they
were, and are, considered — was an irreducible truth of black
life. This is what Bessie Smith is telling us, in *Back-Water Blues*.
This song has as much to do with a flood as *Didn't It Rain* has
to do with Noah, or as *If I Had My Way* has to do with Samson
and Delilah, and poor Samson's excess of hair. Or, if I may
leap again, there is a song being born, somewhere, as I write,
concerning the present "boat-people", which will inform us, in
tremendous detail, how ships are built. There is a dreadful
music connecting the building of ovens with the activity of
contractors, the reality of businessmen (to say nothing of
business) and the reality of bankers and flags, and the
European middle class, and its global progeny, and Gypsies,
Jews, and soap: and profit.

The music called *jazz* came into existence as an exceedingly laconic description of black circumstances: and, as a way, by describing these circumstances, of overcoming them. It was necessary that the description be laconic: the iron necessity being that the description not be overheard. Or, as the indescribably grim remnants of the European notion of the "nation-state" would today put it, it was absolutely necessary that the description not be "de-coded". It has not been "de-coded", by the way, any more than the talking drum has been de-coded. I will try to tell you why.

I have said that people cannot be described from a distance. I will, now, contradict myself, and say that people *can* be described from a distance: the distance that they themselves have established between themselves and what we must, helplessly, here, call life. Life comes out of music, and music comes out of life: without trusting the first, it is impossible to create the second. The rock against which the European notion of the nation-state has crashed is nothing more — and absolutely nothing less — than the question of identity. *Who am I? and what am I doing here?*

This question is the very heart, and root, of the music we are discussing: and contains (if it is possible to make this distinction) not so much a moral judgment as a precise one.

The Irish, for example, as it now, astoundingly, turns out, never had the remotest desire to become English, neither do the people of Scotland, or Wales: and one can suppose that the people of Canada, trapped as they are between Alaska and Mexico, with only the heirs of the doctrine of Manifest Destiny between themselves and these two definitely unknown ports of call, distract themselves with the question of whether they are French or English only because their history has now allowed them the breathing space to find out what in God's name (!) it means to be Canadian. The Basques do not wish to be French, *or* Spanish, Kurds and Berbers do not wish to be Iranian, *or* Turkish.

If one travels from Naples, to Rome, to Torino, it can by no means be taken for granted that the *nation* — hammered into a *nation*, after all, quite recently — ever agreed, among themselves, to be that. The same is true of an equally arbitrary invention, Germany: Bavaria is not Berlin. For that matter, to be in Haifa is not at all like being in Jerusalem, and neither place resembles Nazareth. Examples abound: but, at this moment, the only nations being discussed are those which have become utilitarian but otherwise useless, Sweden, for example, or Switzerland, which is not a nation, but a bank. There are those territories which are considered to be "restive" (Iran, Greece) or those which are "crucial", or "unstable" — or, incomprehensibly, both: Japan, for example, is "crucial", *and* "unstable". Peru, for the moment, is merely "unstable", though one keeps on it a nervous eye: and though we know that there's a whole lot of coffee in Brazil, we don't know who's going to drink it. Brazil threatens to become, as we quite remarkably put it, one of the "emerging" nations, like Nigeria, because those decisions, in those places, involve not merely continents, but the globe. Leaving aside the "crafty East" — China, and Russia — there are only embarrassments, like the British colonial outpost, named for a merciless, piratical *murderer/colonizer*: named Cecil Rhodes.

What, indeed, you may well ask, has all this to do with *The Making of Jazz*? A book concerned, innocently and earnestly enough, with the creation of black American music.

That music is produced by, and bears witness to, one of the most obscene adventures in the history of mankind. It is a music which creates, as what we call History cannot sum up courage to do, the response to that absolutely universal question: *Who am I? what am I doing here?*

How did King Oliver, Ma Rainey, Bessie, Armstrong — a roll-call more vivid than what is called History — Bird, Dolphy, Powell, Pettiford, Coltrane, Jelly-Roll Morton, The Duke — or the living, again, too long a roll-call: Miss Nina Simone, Mme. Mary Lou Williams, Carmen McCrae, The Count, Ray, Miles, Max — forgive me, children, for all the names I cannot call — how did they, and how *do* they, confront that question? and make of that captivity, a song?

For, the music began in captivity: and is, still, absolutely, created in captivity. So much for the European vanity: which imagines that with the single word, *history*, it controls the *past*, defines the *present*: and, therefore, cannot but suppose that the *future* will prove to be as willing to be brought into captivity as the slaves they imagine themselves to have discovered, as the *nigger* they had no choice but to invent.

Be careful of inventions: the invention describes you, and will certainly betray you. Speaking as the son of the Preacher-Man, I know that it was never intended, in any way whatever, that either the Father, or the Son, should be heard. Take that any way you will: I am trying to be precise.

If you know — as a black American *must* know, discovers at his mother's breast, and, then, in the eyes of his father — that the world which calls itself *white*: and which has the further, unspeakable cowardice of calling itself *free* — if you will dare imagine that I, speaking, now, as a black witness to the white condition, see you in a way that you cannot afford to see me: if you can see that the invention of the black condition creates the trap of the white identity: you will see that what a black man *knows* about a white man stems, inexorably, from the white man's description of who, and what, he takes to be the other: in this case, the black cat: me.

You watch this innocent criminal destroying your father, day by day, hour by hour — your *father!* despising your mother, your brothers and your sisters; and this innocent criminal will cut you down, without any mercy, if any one of you dares to say a word about it.

And not only is he trying to kill you. He would also like you to be his accomplice — discreet and noiseless accomplice — in this friendly, democratic, and, alas, absolutely indispensable action. *I didn't*, he will tell you, *make the world.*

You think, but you don't say, to your friendly murderer, who, sincerely, means you no harm: *Well, baby, somebody better. And, in a great big hurry.*

Thus, you begin to see; so, you begin to sing and dance; for, those responsible for your captivity require of you a song. You begin the unimaginable horror of contempt and hatred; then, the horror of self-contempt, and self-hatred. *What did I do? to be so black, and blue?* If you survive — as, for example, the "sociopath", Yard-Bird, did not, as the "junkie", Billie Holiday, did not — you are released onto the tightrope tension of bearing in mind: every hour, every second, drunk, or sober, *in sickness*, or *in health*, those whom you must not even begin to depend on for the truth: and those to whom you must not lie.

It is hard to be black, and, therefore, officially, and lethally, despised. It is harder than that to despise so many of the people who think of themselves as white: before whose blindness you present the obligatory, historical grin.

And it is harder than that, out of this devastation — Ezekiel's valley: *Oh, Lord. Can these bones live?* — to trust life, and to live a life, to love, and be loved.

It is out of this, and much more than this, that black American music springs. This music begins on the auction-block.

Now, whoever is unable to face this — the auction-block: whoever cannot see that that auction-block is the demolition, by Europe, of all human standards: a demolition accomplished, furthermore, at that hour of the world's history, in the name of *civilization*: whoever pretends that the slave mother does not weep, until this hour, for her slaughtered son, that the son does not weep for his slaughtered father: or whoever pretends that the white father did not — literally, and knowing what he was doing — hang, and burn, and castrate, his black son: whoever cannot face this can never pay the price for the *beat* which is the key to music, and the key to life.

Music is our witness, and our ally. The *beat* is the confession which recognises, changes, and conquers time.

Then, history becomes a garment we can wear, and share, and not a cloak in which to hide: and time becomes a friend.

Henry Miller

MOTHER

PREFATORY NOTE

This text was inspired by a dream in which I died and found myself in Devachan (limbo) where I ran into my mother whom I hated all my life.

I DIDN'T quite realise I had died — I seemed so alive — until I saw my mother approaching. Then it struck me that I too must be what we call dead. I hadn't had time to take note of my surroundings; everything seemed so natural even if different.

What immediately struck me was the radiant expression on my mother's face. (That was indeed something new to me.) She looked younger than I had ever known her, even when a boy. She was almost gay.

"O Henry," she exclaimed, as we drew close, "you don't know how glad I am to see you. I waited for you such a long time. What ever kept you on Earth so long?"

A spate of words rushed to my lips but all I could utter was "Mother, dear Mother." Besides, there seemed no necessity for words. I was alive still, but in a new sense. I had a different intelligence, a whole new set of emotions. Above all, I was at peace — in a state of bliss, rather.

"Where are we?" I finally managed to say.

My mother shrugged her shoulders smilingly. "I don't know," she replied. "Nobody ever asks that question. We are content as we are and wherever we are. It is just one vast endless space, and no time, only bits of eternity."

This was a most unusual statement for the mother I knew below to make.

"Mother, you must have learned a lot since you are here," I said.

"Son," she replied, "there is only one thing worse than ignorance and that is stupidity. I don't wonder you couldn't tolerate me down below. I *was* stupid, terribly stupid."

I started to contradict her but she went on talking. "You see, son, all we have to do here is to learn from our past mistakes, so when we are ready to be incarnated again, we will have learned our lesson. We have all time on our hands here. Some learn faster than others and are gone before one really knows them."

"Tell me," I interrupted, "is there any kind of government here?"

"Oh, no," she quickly answered. "There is no need for government here. We are all capable of governing ourselves. You see, one of the first things that happens to you is the loss of all hatred, all bitterness, all prejudice. Besides, there are no nations here. It is just one big world, one big family."

"How do you manage to live, who supplies the food, who does the hard work?"

"There is no work to do," said Mother. "Whatever you wish you get. Wherever you want to go you have only to desire it and you are there — the place comes to you. Do you remember at home in the storm closet there hung a guitar no one ever played? That was *my* guitar — but I had forgotten how to play it. Here I have a guitar anytime I wish it and I can play it well. . . . Just a moment and I will show you." To my amazement in a moment there was a guitar in her hand and she was playing it, skilfully.

"You sound like Segovia," I exclaimed, full of admiration.

"Segovia is here," my mother replied. "I met him and he gave me a few lessons. One learns everything quickly here. The important thing is Desire."

Suddenly it occurred to me my father was not around. When I asked if she knew where he was she said, "Probably in some corner far away. I haven't run into him yet."

"Don't you miss him?" I asked.

"No, son," she said, "I don't miss anybody or anything. One learns to be content here very quickly. Besides, your father may still be drinking his head off, you know. This isn't Heaven. I doubt there is such a place."

"By the way," she added, "I never asked you if you would like something to eat and drink. If you would it can be served to you *instanter*. You can have Chateaubriand with onions and mashed potatoes, if you like. You always loved onions."

"Mother, thank you, I don't want a thing. I feel as if I had everything. Even the air gives sustenance. It's like breathing an elixir. . . . Oh, that reminds me, I don't seem to notice the sky."

"There isn't any," she quickly replied. "I have heard people refer to it as an astral sky. Right now we are in our astral bodies. At least that's what I have been told. But it makes no difference to me what sort of body they call it; it suits me perfectly."

"You mean you never have a toothache or an earache, no constipation, no diarrhoea?"

My mother shook her head vigorously.

"Wouldn't you want to stay here forever?" I inquired.

Again she shook her head. "No, son, our place is on earth. We must go back again and again until it becomes a fit place to live. It would be selfish of me to stay here in this Paradise and leave the earthlings to suffer."

This was indeed a surprising utterance from mother's lips. I had come in a very short space of time not only to like her but to respect and to admire her.

"Mother," I suddenly said, "there is a question on my mind which has been bothering me. Only you can settle it."

"I am not endowed with all wisdom," she said, "but ask me, perhaps I can be of help."

"It's this, mother. When I was in London some years ago a friend of mine took me to meet a medium. He was quite an astonishing man, this medium. I had hardly taken a seat, for example, when he said to me: 'Your books have caused a great deal of trouble, haven't they?' No one had told him that I was a writer. He quickly followed this up by telling me that my greatest helpmate in the beyond was my brother. Did I ever have a brother — perhaps one who died before I was born?"

My mother hesitated a moment or two before replying.

"Son," she said, "that man was right. I had a still-born child before you were born. It was a male child."

"Then he's probably here too," I exclaimed.

"Yes and no," said my mother. "He could have returned to earth already."

A man suddenly approached me and grasped my arm. "You are Henry Miller, aren't you?" he said with a warm smile.

I looked at him but failed to recognise him.

"You wouldn't remember me," he said. "It was long long ago when we met. You were still quite a young man. You gave me a job as a messenger. I had been paroled after ten years in prison for shooting my wife. You listened to my story, put me on the messenger force and advanced me ten dollars out of your own pocket. Do you remember me now?"

I shook my head. That had happened so often I couldn't possibly remember them all. Of a sudden it occurred to me that most of the 100,000 men, women and boys I had interviewed while personnel manager of the telegraph company must be here now. I had probably outlived them all. And with that I began thinking of some of the odd characters I had known during that period.

At this point my mother broke in to tell me she had followed my career as a writer to the very end. "I was so happy for you," she exclaimed. "You wanted so much to be a great writer and after much struggle you succeeded."

"Maybe the medium was right," I remarked. "Maybe my brother did help me along without my ever knowing it."

"Many people here were doing their best to help you," said my mother. "You created a stir even in this world!"

"Mother," I said abruptly, "there's one person I would like very very much to meet if she is still here. Do you remember that first girl I was madly in love with?"

My mother shook her head. "I don't think we've ever met. Probably *she* didn't want to meet me."

"Why do you say that?" I asked.

"Because I was never very sympathetic to any of the women you fell in love with. The truth is, I never thought any of them were good enough for you."

"Mother, how good of you to say that! If only you had told me that when we were below."

"As I told you, son, I was a very stupid woman. And then your father gave me such a hard time."

"Do you still love him?"

"Here we don't love in the fashion of earthlings. We make no distinction between one person and another."

"Doesn't that prove rather dull?"

"Not really. Besides, it helps avoid a lot of anguish."

"Strange," I said, "but I feel quite at home here, yet I've only been here a few minutes. Funny, it ain't Heaven and it ain't Hell. And I don't see no angels flying around or playing the harp."

"There isn't any Heaven or Hell, son. That's all poppycock. And there's no such thing as sin either. That's an invention of the Jews which the Christians adopted and have been poisoning the world with ever since. As for Hell, the real Hell is on Earth."

"Mother, you said the *real* Hell. That's something I wanted to ask you about — everything here seems like a dream."

"You're dead right, son. This is the dream world, the true reality. Down below all is illusion. Only the imagination is real."

She paused a minute to point out two women who were passing.

"See those two," she said. "See those cigarettes dangling from their lips. Well, those are dream cigarettes — they taste like tobacco and smell like tobacco but it's only dream tobacco. They can smoke as many as they like, they'll never get cancer."

So there's no sin and no cancer here, I mused. Wonderful place.

"Don't people get punished here for their misbehaviour?" I asked.

"No, there is no such thing as punishment here. Unless you call it punishment to have nothing to do but think about the mistakes you made while on Earth."

"Yes, mother, I call that severe punishment."

"But it's self-inflicted punishment. There's a difference. You see, son, the universe is run by laws; if you break the law you have to pay the penalty. That's only fair, isn't it? Besides, how are you ever going to learn except through experience? You may have noticed, we have no schools here. Here one acquires wisdom, not learning. We live according to our instincts and our intuitions. Like that we remain part animal, part human. On earth the function of the brain is greatly exaggerated. Think of those foolish scientists who talk about light years and billions of stars. That is sheer nonsense. Here everything is simple and easy to understand. Whoever created the Universe didn't intend life to be a series of crossword puzzles. He made it to be enjoyed. And that's what Jews and Christians find so hard to believe. They wallow in guilt. Even that doesn't make them happy."

"Have you met any Jews since you're here?"

"No, son, I prefer the Negroes, the Pygmies, the Zulus. They are such wonderful, joyous people. And where they lived on earth they had almost nothing.

"You know," she continued, "when I get born again, I hope I am going to be male and black. I get along with those people famously."

I couldn't help but smile. Mother had come a long way from the woman I knew on Earth.

"How long do you think you still have to stay here?" I asked.

"It's up to me when to leave. When I've picked the family I want to be born in and the environment. When I'm ready for another go around."

"I hope that won't be soon, mother. I'd feel lost without you."

"No you wouldn't," she said quickly. "That's one of the first things you learn on arriving here. Self-reliance. No more loneliness. Wherever you go you're at home. Whomever you meet is your friend."

I wondered if she ever encountered souls from other planets. And if so, in what language they communicated. I was not too surprised when she said of course they met souls from other planets — even from other universes. They weren't so very different from earthlings — perhaps the eyes were more brilliant and the mind sharper. But though the people from outer space could understand the people here, the latter could not understand the people from outer space.

(I forgot to say the people here understood all earth languages though they might not speak them. It was as if they had received the gift of tongues.)

From what little I could gather about the people of outer space it would seem there was nothing so very mysterious about the universe; the mystery was Man, wherever he might be. *That* made a great impression on me. So then possibly there was something to the biblical saying, that man was made in the image of the Creator! And consequently an enigma to himself!

After hearing so much from her lips that made sense to me I decided to ask her outright why she had always been so cold to me. I particularly wanted to know why she never had a word of comfort for me when she knew my heart was breaking. Couldn't she help me locate Cora now, I wondered. No, the only way to find someone here was to think hard, wish for them and they would appear. She thought it quite possible that Cora had already returned to Earth.

"She was a good girl," she said, "only I didn't see very much in her. I knew you were suffering, but I felt that you had to work it out yourself. I always believed in letting people do as they wish, even if they wanted to kill themselves."

I decided to say no more about Cora but to try to find her on my own.

My mother, however, ventured to add a few more words. "The real place to look for her," she said, "is on Earth. That's the whole purpose of love — to find your other half. Sometimes the search goes on for a thousand years."

These observations bowled me over. "Why mother," I exclaimed, "you sound as if you had read Marie Corelli."

"Marie Corelli . . . Marie Corelli . . .," she repeated a few times. "Why yes, son, that name strikes a familiar chord. I *did* read her when I was in my teens. I remember one book especially — *A Romance of Two Worlds*. Everybody was reading it then. She was all the rage." She paused for a moment. "Why do you ask me about her? Have you read her too?"

"Indeed I have, I rediscovered her towards the end of my life. She meant a great deal to me. Mother, do you think she might be *here*? She only died about fifty years ago."

"I have no idea," mother replied. "But I told you how to find the ones you are looking for."

Her words made me jubilant. How lucky I was, I thought, to be here where so many of my favourite writers were. Maybe they had a club or formed a community of their own. I would look not only for Marie Corelli, but for Dostoievsky, Knut Hamsun, Herman Hesse. In this realm I had more chance of meeting those I wanted to meet than on Earth.

But I was not through questioning my mother about the things which had estranged us in life. I realised, of course, from the moment I encountered her that she was an entirely different person here. How good it was to exchange thoughts with her. Below we hardly spoke to one another.

"Mother," I began, "do you remember a woman I wanted to marry who was considerably older than myself? Do you recall the day I told you about her — we were sitting in the kitchen — and you took a big carving knife and threatened to plunge it into me if I said another word about marriage? If, as you said a moment ago, you believed in letting people do as they wish, why did you become so furious, so violent?"

"Because," she replied, "you were out of your mind. It was only an infatuation, not true love.

"However," she added, "you did go and live with her a few

years, even if you didn't marry her. And they were years of torment and distress, weren't they?"

I shook my head affirmatively. "But mother, no matter if it were an infatuation, she was a good woman. You should have felt a little compassion for her."

For answer she replied, "Sometimes one runs out of compassion. The world below was so full of misery that if one felt sorry for everyone who was in distress one could shed rivers of tears. When I return to Earth this time I am sure I shall have more courage and strength than before."

Having endured much suffering, misery, humiliation, I could appreciate her words. I had one more vital question to put to her.

"Mother," I began, "I have never been able to believe that you preferred to see me become a tailor rather than a writer. Was that true or did you have some other reason?"

"I'm only too glad you asked me that question. Of course I never meant to imply a tailor was more important than a writer. (Though I must confess that since being here I have arrived at the conclusion that one thing is no better than another. I have met some very wonderful souls here, and they were people of no account on Earth.) But I am wandering afield. I wanted you to be with your father, to guide him and protect him. I couldn't bear to see him go to the dogs. That's the real reason I wanted you to be a tailor."

"I suspected as much," I answered. "But mother, why did you refuse to read anything I had written?"

"Son, father told me about your books and I just didn't want to read such language coming from you. I knew, when you were just a boy, that you had the makings of a writer. Don't you remember all the books I gave you each Christmas? I used to envy you having all those wonderful books to read. From the time I married your father I never had the time to even glance at a book."

"Poor mother," I said. "And I was foolish enough to think you didn't care about books. How stupid of me!"

She looked at me tenderly and said: "Since I am here I've

discovered that books aren't as important as we believe on earth. We have no newspapers, magazines or books. I would say that in talking to one another we are reading and writing books. And we don't get headaches and colitis from it either. Every day we gain a broader outlook on life, become more tolerant and more at peace with ourselves and one another."

"I wish some writers I know could have heard your words. How beautifully put! Now I see where I got my talent from! It was always a mystery to me, always bothered me. I used to console myself by saying that often geniuses are born of very ordinary parents. What egotism!"

Whereupon my mother observed, "Nobody has an easy time of it on earth. Earth is the testing ground. And, as I remarked before, it is close to being Hell. The torment, the poverty, the misery of mankind seems like the vengeance of some cruel god. Here we don't talk of God or gods. Neither did the Buddha, if you remember his words!"

I was becoming more and more impressed with my mother's words. Far from being a dumbbell I found wisdom in her words. Had she perhaps mingled with some of the great writers of the past? There must be many of them here, I thought to myself. But as I soon found out, the best ones had long since returned to earth. Some souls remained only a week or a month, while others stayed for centuries. Thus I soon discovered Dostoievsky, Tolstoi, Walt Whitman, Knut Hamsun and a few other of my great favourites were no longer in limbo. They had learned fast. I could have Hemingway, Sinclair Lewis, Waldo Frank and the like, even Jack London, but I passed it up.

Knowing my preoccupation with literature, she indicated a certain corner where they usually congregated, but I didn't bother to go. Somehow I was learning more and enjoying myself more, just conversing with my mother. I had abandoned the idea of finding my father. He and Barrymore, his drinking companion below, had probably ferreted out a jolly bar in some out of the way corner.

It is generally assumed that one doesn't know he is dead

until some time after his expiration. That certainly was true in my case. Of course, as I have remarked earlier, there is no such thing as time here. Just as one never sees a school house, a radio or television set, a telephone, so one never sees a time piece. Five minutes may seem like a year and a hundred years like a few days. Also, to be sure, there is no sign of automobile or train. The sky is utterly different — more like the Mediterranean and the stars shine brightly day and night. Wildlife is also missing, but the air is filled with birds of all kinds, all colours, usually. Singing melodiously. The ground is studded with wild flowers gleaming like rubies, sapphires, emeralds. At the horizon the edges curl up, giving the impression of being inside a limitless pancake. Fatigue is almost unknown, as this astral body is one which never wears out. A very noticeable thing is no one seems to be in a hurry. Nothing has great importance or urgency. Everything seems natural, extremely natural. One is at home and at peace immediately. The scholars and scientists, with their burning questions and dubious theories here partake of a seeming eternal rest.

I had a premonition that my mother was getting ready to return to Earth. I asked her how would we recognise one another when I too returned to Earth. She said there was no way. One only *felt* that one had known another in a previous existence. As she spoke I recalled all the things I had heard on earth about reincarnation, karma, and so on. Nearly everyone I knew had experienced some strange "coincidence" at some time or other in his life. Many is the time, in a foreign country, that I had walked the same street before, recognised every house on the block. Also it frequently happened that I ran into someone and knew them instantly. Maybe we had last met in Egypt or China or Africa. Despite all the arguments of cynics and disbelievers, the existence of the soul, the eternality of life, was well known to earthlings. If there was such a thing as Hell on Earth there was also "Snatches of other realities". Was "reality" not the very word philosophers and metaphysicians quarreled about? Yet it often happened that a simple ignorant peasant or a so-called fool knew more about such matters than the wise ones. However much I wanted to meet Cora again, I began to feel more and more that I would elect to return to some other planet rather than Earth. Though I had made the best of a difficult life, though I had learned to transform the bad into the good, still I felt that Earth had nothing more to offer me. If possible, I would not only choose another planet but another Universe! I was no longer looking for approbation but for confirmations.

Reflecting on the absence of such figures as Marie Corelli and Rider Haggard, I began to suspect that they too had elected for a different world than the one they came from.

The one thing I prayed I would never witness again was violence. A world without crime, without war or revolution, without sickness and poverty, without bitterness and prejudice seemed to my way of thinking like the only real Heaven. Let the dead kill the dead, I said to myself. Crazy as it sounds, it made great sense to me. Not a single one of us had had a real chance on Earth. Even the rich were miserable. Even the men of genius suffered tribulations of all kinds. Nor had the good ones been spared. It was as if the planet were diseased, or condemned. *Un monde maudit.* No wonder the brilliant ones were the poets, the madmen like Blake and Rimbaud. No wonder everything was topsy-turvy. No wonder man was beginning to explore outer space — to find new homes for a dwindling humanity, a humanity that had killed the mother which bore it.

The crime of hating my mother while alive now seemed to me enormously significant. I was indeed, as I had written in some book, "a traitor to the human race". The only escape for me was to quit the planet once and for all, find another Heaven and Earth, another God or gods. It seemed utterly inconsequential now to seek out my beloved authors. I knew now they could give me no comfort, no wisdom. The whole business of literature seemed a completely futile one.

If my mother was ready to leave I certainly was not. There was so much I had to discover — perhaps I would be detained a thousand years. All the better, thought I to myself. Perhaps it will be a new Heaven and a new Earth everywhere, in all the Universes.

During these reflections my mother had skipped from sight unknown to me. I looked about me but could see no trace of her. Had she already returned to Mother Earth? The mere thought of such a possibility filled me with a profound sadness. I sank to the ground and held my head in my hands.

When I looked up I perceived my mother some distance away. She appeared to be on her way out. Looking more carefully, I observed that she was waving to me, waving goodbye.

With that I stood up, my eyes wet with tears, and giving a mighty shout, I cried: "Mother, I love you. *I love you!* Do you hear me?"

I imagined that I saw a faint smile illumine her face and then suddenly she was no more.

I was alone, but more alone than I had ever felt on Earth. And I would be alone, perhaps, for centuries or, who knows, perhaps through all eternity.

Norman MacCaig

INVASION OF BEES

Between the ceiling and the roof
whole fields were humming.

Or, add to one bee a thousand others and it becomes
a dynamo.

A man was fetched from Helmsdale.
He carried a vicious brass pump.

It switched off that dynamo, it reaped
whole fields and heather slopes.

And a summer inside the summer
died, leaving a useless crop.

I have a summer inside my summer.
I cherish it. It's flowery and heathery.

Terrified, I dream of a man from Helmsdale
walking towards me, a sack in his hand.

Gerald Mangan

GLASGOW, 1956

There's always a headscarf stooped
into a pram, nodding in time
with a plastic rattle, outside a shop
advertising a sale of wallpaper.

There's a queue facing another queue
like chessmen across the street—
a hearse standing at a petrol pump
as the chauffeur tests the tyres,

the undertaker brushes ash off
his morning paper, and my mother,
is telling me not to point.

The background is a level site
where we recreate the war.
Calder Street is Calder Street,
level as far as the Clyde.

Without a tree to denote it,
the season is moot. That faint
thunder is the Cathcart tram,
and the sky is white as a trousseau

posed against blackened bricks.
A grey posy in her hands,
the bride stands smiling there
for decades, waiting for the click.

Sean O'Brien

THE BEAT GOES ON

The radio's remembering
Piano-shifting brutalists
In suits of whorish pink, who vocalise
Bluenote-bayous of razz and grief; remembering
Mulatto chords and Mama Roux,
The currency and then the price
The obeah man exacts
For stealing shellac masters
From the tombs of Creole Pharaohs
Still cool in their coke-filled sarcophagi
Under the boardwalks of Hell; remembering
The life you never lived
Again, a riding cymbal-shimmer
Hit with a hickory Premier C
As the horns stand up in the key of real sex.
Encyclopaedias of air encode
The glamour of the singing poor.
We learn them like a second heart.
They gave the mirror all its moves:
Tonight it will not even laugh—
And for this I have drummed out the grease
From a lifetime of antimacassars,
Nagged by good taste and a future
That looks as high and lonesome now
As a busload of drunks and their delicate axes
Marooned in the snowy sierras.

There's no cenotaph for those
Who try to cut the cost of touring,
Who go in derailments, in cropdusters' biplanes,
To Klansmen at crossroads,
Shot down by their mistreated girls
Or drowned in concrete by the mob,
And they cannot now honour their contract
To make us a language of passion and style.
But this evening the King,
So bored he even broadcasts hymns
To the wives of Nebraska and Kansas,
Who sweat at the prospect of leisure
And choke on their sociables, feeling him move
On the air over wheatfields and highways.
The King keeps his class in the bathroom
With the whips and methadone.
He turns the Baptist Gospel off
And hears the Princes practice down the hall.
They are harder and blacker and closer to jail
And the heartbreaking four forty-nine.
Tonight the trailer park gets drunk
Beneath a moon of impotence
As someone seminal awakes
At the wheel of a stolen Chevrolet,
To search the airwaves once again
For something that could make him dance,
With whisky freezing on his shirt
And a writ for his skin in his pocket.

Douglas Dunn

HUGH MacDIARMID:
Inhuman Splendours

FOR a number of reasons, all rather like those held against Ezra Pound, few pundits have been seen not to have resisted or ignored Hugh MacDiarmid's poetry and ideas. His poetry is of itself resistant. It works up a dauntingly national concern, in language, politics, culture and history, far more exacerbated than Yeats's. Non-Scottish readers of goodwill may well have experienced that aspect of MacDiarmid as calculated to put them off, or as none of their business.

Part of this book's* function is to show why *The Age of MacDiarmid* is a true token of his importance to those involved in Scottish literature and Scottish life in general. But local explanations of MacDiarmid's literary, intellectual, political and cultural foundations offer grounds for alarm as well as approval. Although MacDiarmid lived by principles of permanent opposition, it could prove monstrously disabling if Scottish critics were to become rutted in gestures either of permanent evangelism or permanent explication of one incontestably major figure. What we need now are books, not essays in salesmanship.

MacDiarmid's poetry poses a primary critical embarrassment — much of it is extraordinarily good, a lot of it is peculiarly bad. For every convincing passage of writing there are pages and pages of dogmatic absurdity; for each beautiful lyric, each memorable excerpt from *A Drunk Man Looks at the Thistle*, there are scores of sloppy instances to set against it.

* *The Age of MacDiarmid*, edited by P. H. Scott and A. C. Davis. (Edinburgh, 1981)

Too many critics take MacDiarmid's volcanic fire-and-lava self-portrait at its face value. There are other embarrassments, too — of politics especially, and of a personality that was all too typical of the 1920s and 1930s: like Lawrence and Pound, he claimed to be objective and authoritative, when he was subjective and totalitarian. If, then, the title of this collection seems right, I want to know exactly what I am acknowledging. In an appraisal of Hugh MacDiarmid, the work and the man, no one should give the impression of accepting what he does not believe; and, at the opposite extreme, a writer should keep cool in the face of MacDiarmid's real and imaginary ideologies. The trouble in writing about MacDiarmid is that there are (or should be) so many suspensions of disbelief to hold in perspective, that it can look as if you are dismissing his poetry and ideas instead of trying to understand them.

Kenneth Buthlay comes close to an exemplary coolness in his guide to MacDiarmid's use of sources in *To Circumjack Cencrastus*. MacDiarmid, Buthlay concludes, "over-relied" on his reading as the staple of his long poems. How damaging a criticism is that? Mr Buthlay is discriminating, showing us the extent to which MacDiarmid transcended, or, in the fullest sense of the word, incorporated his second-hand material. It may be wise, therefore, to refrain from judging the force of that "over-reliance" until such time as a "brass-bowelled" scholar (as David Murison calls this awaited annotator) gives us a full account of MacDiarmid's reading and quotation. This, too, has been an embarrassment to MacDiarmid's work, ever since that correspondence about his liftings which ran from January to May 1965 in the *T.L.S.* MacDiarmid's attitude then to his poem "Perfect" was that "any plagiarism was certainly not conscious". In a late interview on television with Ludovic Kennedy, however, he boasted of his skill as a plagiarist. In the meantime, before an annotated edition appears (if it ever does) I suggest the usefulness of Emerson's essay on "Quotation and Originality" (available in *The Portable Emerson*, Penguin). Once well known, Emerson's essay will show something of MacDiarmid's sagacity as well as a psychology from which a reliance on other men's wisdom is built. It is surprising that Mr Buthlay does not draw from it.

Performing hand-wringing exercises over "On a Raised Beach", Iain Crichton Smith comes as near as the book gets to indignation. At times he looks as if on the verge of rejecting the poem. "Such a poetry," he says, "allows the mind to construct opposites for what is being said." It has "an intention aimed at us" and is "a poetry of propaganda and persuasion". Yet "On a Raised Beach" can be read as an intellectual drama, a discovery of *vita nuova*, in which intent and persuasion are directed as much to the poet himself as to his reader. It can be read as an attempt by the poet to reduce himself and to be consoled by his reduction to the phenomena he evokes, in the hope of growth and purification. Much of the poem's diction gets in the way: the scene becomes a geological blur instead of the non-romantic, precise and scientific description it was perhaps meant to be. When MacDiarmid says that he is "prepared with everything else to share/Sunshine and darkness and wind and rain", it is a release through contemplation, into "a more than Roman peace", and into a lyric moment. This is traditional, so much part of a standard poetic experience, that it is hopeless to find fault with it, as Mr Smith does not, for that, precisely, is the moment where MacDiarmid relinquishes the methodology which got him there and engenders a shared form of expression. What I find worrying about the poem — and I am surprised that Mr Smith says nothing of this — is the puritanical, fist-clenching, spartan nature of the instruction MacDiarmid takes from stones.

> By what immense exercise of will,
> Inconceivable discipline, courage and endurance,
> Self-purification and anti-humanity,
> Be ourselves without interruption,
> Adamantine and inexorable?

Here, then, is a poet who willed, whose self-purification led him to step beyond the human realm, and who wished to be "adamantine and inexorable". Cynically, these meditations look like mere toughening-up. More to the point, however, is the public and private history of the 1920s and 1930s against which the poem was written. It was an age of intentions, propagandas and persuasions. Implicated in "On a Raised Beach", at a lower level of consciousness, is the vulnerability of those beset by the impact of contending philosophies, as well as the rock-like arrogance of others who believed in them, first one, then another, Fascism and Socialism, and who participated in their meanings. MacDiarmid's fiery but remote temper led him to outbursts such as "To Hell wi' happiness!", followed by these lines from *To Circumjack Cencrastus*, which Buthlay shows were versified from Valéry's prose:

> I sing the terrifying discipline
> O' the free mind that gars a man
> Mak' his joys kill his joys,
> The weakest by the strongest,
> The temporal by the fundamental....

Private motives, contributing to this, in his own word "inhuman" stance of the artist, were probably as important as the public ideologies from which MacDiarmid drew, from 1923 onwards, until by the time of his "exile" on Whalsay, he began to make a virtue of what may otherwise have been a psychologically unattractive form of self-regard.

The contrast between MacDiarmid's early attitude to his poetry — "Wee bit sangs are a' I need" (*Penny Wheep*, 1926) — and his latter-day prescription, "I am all for GIANTISM in the arts", is pointed out in the essay by David Daiches. Of this transformation, or upheaval and reversal of literary practice, as well as of beliefs, Daiches comes up with the formula of "self-contradiction as a mode of poetic awareness". What has to be kept in mind, though, is the punishing commitment with which he held each phase of creativity and each new idea or cause or new modification introduced to improve them. That, surely, shows "self-contradiction" in MacDiarmid as more extreme, more than Whitmanesque; and it should serve to remind us of the extent to which MacDiarmid's searching mind penetrated the most contradictory aesthetic and political views of the century, as if determined to be exhaustive. His poetry ranges from scones, in "Country Life", to a notion of "A poetry like the hope of achieving ere very long/A tolerable idea of what happens from first to last", in *The Kind of Poetry I Want*.

There is no virtue in being always where extremes meet when these are, politically, MacDiarmid's Fascism of 1923 (no one in the book refers to this, with documentation, I see), his alarming use of Nazi cultural ciphers in the 1930s, his sometimes racist Nationalism, and his Stalinism, to which he drew public attention in 1956-57. Quirks of personality can make an aptitude for extremity look like a hideous ploy; it can appear as a tactic, isolating the believer as strong, incorrigible, authoritative, as an Old Man of the Mountains whose intellectual superiority forbids him to have so much as the time of day for the common man lest he compromise his iron resolve with a lapse of "humanity". By any standards, MacDiarmid went through, not one fanaticism, but a series of them, sometimes moving in an ensemble of fanatical fronts. Self-contradiction? No. Even the brave and the brilliant can be stupid.

Professor Daiches quotes these lines:

> And I lo'e Love
> Wi' a scunner in 't.

"For MacDiarmid," writes Daiches, "the mystic trance always has a scunner in it." It is probably true; but it does not comment on these lines. MacDiarmid wrote that he loves Love with a scunner in it. It is candid, and it is "modern", but it ripples through MacDiarmid's attitudes to other things as well, and it seems to have its origin in as intimate, as personal a state of mind as an attitude towards Love.

"There is a discipline here," says Daiches, considering MacDiarmid's submission to a language of "facts", "the discipline of impersonality, which is something central to

MacDiarmid's mature work." Why, then, do I find MacDiarmid's later poetry markedly egocentric? Where Daiches finds impersonality, I see a theoretical concern for disinterestedness obstructed by a particularity of self. Fear of self is perhaps a reason for transcendence or the attempted achievement of impersonality. To call it mystical is to refuse to acknowledge the motives of that process as human. What happens in such a use of imagination is that Man is abandoned to the mercy of an imaginatively perceived cosmos. MacDiarmid, bolstering his poems up with facts, pretends that his method is less speculative, less tentative than it is. It results in a total scunner, a revulsion for trivialities, for the ordinariness of life.

> So I am delivered from the microscopic human chaos
> And given the perspective of a writer who can draw
> The wild disorder of a ship in a gale
> Against the vaster natural order of sea and sky.
> If a man does not bulk too big in his rendering
> He does not lose the larger half of dignity either.

That deliverance might be thought to bulk pretty large in MacDiarmid's rendering. From his lyrics, though, especially "The Bonnie Broukit Bairn" and "The Eemis Stane", or in his colloquially panoptic *A Drunk Man Looks at the Thistle*, that "vaster natural order" was *intuitively* perceived. Through *To Circumjack Cencrastus*, to *In Memoriam James Joyce* (1955) and *The Kind of Poetry I Want*, he extended that early, pure lyrical intuition into realms of assertion, facts and alleged proofs. Politics, nationalism, Scotland, economics, linguistics, sciences, abstruse international literature — the more these became his materials, the further he went into adversary Modernism. Edmund Wilson has a phrase about "the dark crossroads where literature and politics meet". In MacDiarmid's case, the crossroads may be dark, but it looks like Spaghetti Junction.

Obviously, MacDiarmid's attempted deliverance from "microscopic human chaos" is heroic. But from the character of his work, poem after poem, his heroism looks willed. It looks as if he set up a series of obstacles like thick hedges to be barged through as tests to prove his intellectual courage. Why does a man wish his life, his work, his name, to be such that they can be described as "adamantine" and "inexorable". It looks a strange desire, as well as an uncommonly heroic one, to those of us who avoid danger and distress, but who hope to confront them with dignity when they arrive, as they do, in the course of circumstances. Lionel Trilling writes somewhere that literature depends on "that interplay between free will and circumstance" which politics and other assumptions crush. We need not go that far and still distrust, as potential manufacturers of slaughterhouses and secondhand uniforms, all those who brace unjustifiable risks, who say we should do as they do or else look puny, half-hearted, bloodless and unmanned. MacDiarmid is as preacherly and as convinced as Lawrence; he is as relentless and as unforgiving as Pound. An essential meaning of Modernism is that life is potential, its beauty withheld by mistaken social and spiritual assumptions. Like Pound and Lawrence, MacDiarmid observed actuality as a scunner, as sickening and stupid, and saw all men, with the exceptions of a few confrères, as idiots, and the masses as a despicable *canaille*.

Beyond a doubt, MacDiarmid was the most incautious of poets and, in a way that I cannot help but think was reckless, the most valiant. Adjectives like "reckless", however, are of the sort which it seems we must keep to ourselves when writing about MacDiarmid. Evident throughout this book is a subordination of critical energy to a sense of occasion, the occasion being MacDiarmid himself. Duncan Glen delivers a minor homily, a testament to MacDiarmid's influence on him — chasing up books, exchanging letters and, at last, meetings with the Great Man: no admissions here that there might be something conspicuously squalid in MacDiarmid's work to set alongside his marvels. Even so well-rehearsed a critic as David Daiches holds back: incautious poets, it seems, encourage an excess of critical tact. At least he mentions MacDiarmid's

awful rhymes — "the period in review", he quotes, rhymed
with "homes that would make swine spew". This, he says,
"belongs to another order of writing". Indeed it does; and, as
there is more of that in MacDiarmid — much more, with its
equivalent in unrhymed free verse — a paragraph or two on the
status of MacDiarmid's ratt-rhyme and verbose rambles, if
status they have, would have served us better. "The fact is,"
Neal Ascherson writes in his essay "MacDiarmid and
Politics", "that we take MacDiarmid at Grieve's own
valuation still, and have found no important grounds to
question it." He is referring to "Arthur Leslie's" review of
"Hugh MacDiarmid", not MacDiarmid's poetry, but even so
it is bad enough that so concussively hagiographical a
statement should appear in a contribution about
MacDiarmid's politics, while it is practically inexplicable that
it should come from a political analyst as good as Mr
Ascherson usually is in other contexts. On the other hand
Ascherson is aware of the murkier concepts MacDiarmid
picked up from time to time. Fuss has been made over Pound's
and Eliot's anti-Semitic slip-ups. Here is one of MacDiarmid's,
from about 1932/33:

> Brooding again on Edinburgh, that unparalleled
> Provision for noble functions all unfulfilled,
> Mere factor to London now, and Jewry, for the land
> That would have been its own if it had rightly willed. . . .

Pound-like excrescences of diction portray what
MacDiarmid's mind was going through: "dung-beetles of
Empire"; "lice-like jewels"; "impenetrable filth". "Queer
company for a Marxist to keep," Mr Ascherson concludes,
commenting on one astounding remark, one "choking
mouthful of hot ideology" after another. Mr Ascherson fails to
be seen choking on them. And the reason why is explained by
the occasion. Like other contributors, he rises to a flight of
reprehensible rhetoric at the end of his essay: all is forgiven in a
sleight of sententiousness.

"Towards the dying Gaelic civilisation of the islands,"

writes Owen Dudley Edwards, MacDiarmid showed "perhaps, rather more romanticism: but his work on it asserted the totality that he brought to the understanding of the Scotland he wished to liberate and redeem." It is very savoury, that "perhaps". A cooler view of MacDiarmid's "Gaelic Idea" shows it up as a fantasy — he promoted its global ramifications as well as its national significance, while his vision of Scotia Irrendenta (England north of the Humber), and of a federation of Celtic republics, amount to wishful-thinking just as bogus. MacDiarmid, says Edwards, "*was* recalling his people to a God of Scotland to whom they had turned their backs in order to achieve preferred provincial status in the spiritual empire of Baal". Heady stuff, indeed; but Edwards fails to suggest that MacDiarmid saw *himself* as that God. "I am Scotland itself today," he states, in "The Difference", written at about the time when he was banished from the Scottish National Party. Without criticism, with no reservations whatsoever, Stephen Maxwell quotes from "The Poet as Prophet" in his essay on "MacDiarmid and Nationalism":

> Scotland felt at that moment
> That no man ever personified her,
> Ever would represent her,
> As he did
> And she grew in glory
> And was transfigured with pride.
> It was not a Scottish moment;
> It was a universal moment.

Admittedly, a little dramatic licence may withhold a total self-identification of MacDiarmid with "The man for whom Gaeldom is waiting", which is the subtitle of the poem. Yet it is hard to avoid that the association of himself with Gaeldom is as sentimental as Kailyard bucolics written by rich bourgeois, or Jacobite songs penned by aristocratic married ladies. Nor is it acceptable to try to safeguard the "unity of his thought", which is a piety for the occasion: the individual parts of

MacDiarmid's thought are frightening. Whether the result of carelessness, or of messianic or daemonic desire, there are times when MacDiarmid looks an armchair Führer, casting his eyes round for sheep to lead. I submit that MacDiarmid appeals not only to the bookishness of Scotsmen when he is proving his erudition, but that when he is testifying to his temperament, his vituperation, his muscular tantrums, when he flaunts his anti-democratic moods, then he appeals to the very worst thing in the Scots make-up, our hypothetical, do-anything-if-we-are-well-led, cursing, mawkish, loud-mouthed militarism, the braggart's quinsy. He pretends to be the Omnipotent Kiltie, and is covered up by disciples who say he is being no more than earnestly capricious.

* * *

The experience of reading MacDiarmid's poetry is to begin with a wholehearted surrender to his lyrics, and to *A Drunk Man Looks at the Thistle.* As his work grows and takes new directions, then the stimulus or irritation of his poetry leads to many turnings back in the two fat volumes of *The Complete Poems.* It is to experience despair as well as exhilaration, offence as well as delight. Swathes of what come to look predictable are redeemed by outbursts of surprise. The longer this reading goes on, the more ruthless, eccentric or lunatic ideas become taken for granted. Self-contradiction begins to look almost like the poetic mode Professor Daiches claims for it. Yet the convictions which are put down and the new ones which take their place are always controversial. It is a difficult body of work to live with at all comfortably. At every stage it challenges preconceived literary taste.

Sorley Maclean contributes a remarkable testimony to the influence of MacDiarmid's lyrics on his work. They were like "red lights stopping my way of poetry". Mr Maclean is referring to those spoken but song-like and enharmonious perfections of *Sangschaw* and *Penny Wheep*, the *diapason chordon* of Scottish poetry, or these "ineluctable" lyrics (as Maclean calls them).

119

Elsewhere I have called MacDiarmid's early lyrics in Scots a poetry of "felt philology", a form of sentient erudition. It is the more remarkable in that its lexical originality exists within the innovations of the forms he used. Owen Dudley Edwards points to the Victorian origins of MacDiarmid's prose, and it is worth bearing in mind that *Sangschaw* and *Penny Wheep* amount to a reckoning with an unsatisfactory literary past and present as much as Eliot's poetry, or Pound's, that same emergence from the nineteenth century, even if a corresponding revolution did not interest MacDiarmid as a prose writer. In an article which otherwise indulges in more self-advertisement than might be decent, Alan Bold indicates convincingly MacDiarmid's break with verse forms that had come to be associated with Kailyard poetry. Many of the lyrics, however, *are* in quatrains, although with a shortening of the line, while a poem like "The Watergaw", with its six-line stanza, may merge subconsciously both quatrain and Standard Habbie. In any case, the effects of his earlier lyric poems are strikingly close to those of the ballads, with their *frissons*, with (in MacDiarmid's case) telescoped narratives, their characters, with alterations of the robust and the delicate and a marked evocation of death and strangeness.

David Murison regrets in his informative article on "The Language Problem" that poems like "By Wauchopeside" and "Whuchulls" did not come to form the stylistic ground of what MacDiarmid wrote after his lyrics of the 1920s. MacDiarmid himself seems to have had that course in mind. Although extended, both are lyric poems, as Mr Murison says, but he is also aware of how their sentiments prefigure such poems as "On a Raised Beach". Without noticing these longer lyrics, Professor Daiches observes that MacDiarmid leapt from the inspired control of his lyrics, and from what Daiches calls, in a splendid phrase, the "ordered loquacity" of *A Drunk Man Looks at the Thistle*, to the "large, unstructured verse-paragraph". Yet MacDiarmid's "verse-paragraph" poems differ from each other. "England is Our Enemy", for instance, is a plainer "essay", more open to uninterrupted if thoughtful reading than most of *In Memoriam James Joyce*. In style, it is to that book much as "Island Funeral" is to the tenser, more lexically synthetic "On a Raised Beach". Also, a good many of MacDiarmid's poems of the 1930s *are* stanzaic or metrical, at least in parts. Metrical procedures often look as if they are being set up for the poem as a whole, but then take off in different directions, sometimes as free verse, sometimes metrical again and sometimes lyric. The technical uncertainty of a poem like "Ode to all Rebels", for example, may even be a function of the uneasy relationship between the poem's marital fictions and what we know (or think we know) of MacDiarmid's life at the time.

He lamented his "double life and double tongue — guid Scots wi' English a' hamstrung", knowing his English as his language of daily use and Scots "the true language o' my thochts" long before that strikingly similar passage in Edwin Muir's *Scott and Scotland* (1936) led him into a disgraceful condemnation of his old friend and supporter. George Bruce deals very adequately with the relationship between Muir and MacDiarmid.

In spite of his vindictiveness on that occasion, MacDiarmid could be unremittingly generous and encouraging. Accounts of the man portray him as extraordinary and agreeable. There is a passage on page 851 of *The Complete Poems*, "The Snares of Varuna" section of *In Memoriam James Joyce*. It shows what does appear the true, more relaxed side of MacDiarmid's personality, the side with which his ideologies interfered. He talks of angling, and of telling Norman MacCaig that if he, MacDiarmid, went fishing, then he could not be content with a trout or salmon. Instead, he lists big, exotic, fierce and legendary fish.

> And MacCaig has laughed and said
> "Let me see you catch anything yet
> Big enough not to throw in again."

This is probably the real personality of MacDiarmid but it appears rarely in his poetry. What, then, are the reasons for his dogmatic, ultra-passionate, and caricatured commitments to his beliefs? A fundamental antagonism to mass democratic society is reiterated and detailed in his poetry. To some extent it can be understood as a natural consequence of how his own cultural reality was at odds with the reality of Scotland as a whole. It may amount to nothing more than "self-contradiction", but it is interesting to notice how he assaulted Roy Campbell in *The Battle Continues*, berating Campbell for lacking qualities which, in earlier poetry, he was at pains to disclaim he possessed himself or that he placed any value on them whatsoever:

> The further society draws away, Campbell,
> From the fundamentals of Christianity,
> From peace, from love of one's neighbour, from charity,
> The more receptive it becomes
> To doctrines like Hitler's, Mussolini's, Franco's, yours.
> —Doctrines which are a declaration of war
> Against the basis of our intellectual and moral existence;
> A crude, wild, outrageous attack on humanity
> Before the so-called conflict
> Between Christianity and Socialism pales into insignificance.

Surveying MacDiarmid's Scotland, Edwin Morgan is on safe ground when directing us to MacDiarmid's satires on the decline of the Scottish character, hateful laird-like types, unions, philistines or the cult of the wee, the funny and the sentimental. More controversial, however, is MacDiarmid's estimate of Glasgow and the industrial west of Scotland.

> To see or hear a clock in Glasgow's horrible,
> Like seeing a dead man's watch, still going, though he's dead.
> Everything is dead except stupidity here.

The force of these lines (albeit derived from Rilke) proves the truth of MacDiarmid's revulsion. Yet I feel that it is exaggerated, that it is the emotional counterpart of his "Ecclefechan Gongorism" — that euphuistic, exaggerated writing invented by Luis de Gongora y Argote (1561-1627).

And he, too, I see, "aroused strong feelings of devotion or detestation, and he revelled in conflict". So much in MacDiarmid is a matter of dismissal (Harry Lauder, ministers, J. M. Barrie *et al*), or of panoptic visions of the past and future. Strikingly absent in his work is a detailed understanding of the present, what people do, how they live, and yet he seems to have been well placed to provide that basis for his generalised assumptions. He could not see Glasgow as a monolithic victim, man-made and infertile, the created opposite to what may be seen and felt on Highland mountain-tops, or lived in the cosiness of small towns and farms. Nowhere in his writing that I know of does he depict, at any length, a disinterested urban scene. In "Island Funeral" and many other shorter poems he could evoke the lives of rural communities or individuals, people hardly touched by what he felt had corrupted Glasgow into the status of an unthinking monster.

The antithesis in his work — of country preferred to town — is of a piece with the imagination from which his marvellous lyrics flowed. In these, his melodious, exciting lexis can still stir whatever residual native psyche is left to us, but it is a writing that rekindles fires that in truth went out a long time ago in the hearths of our fathers and grandfathers. They burn only in the imagination, but even there they amount to a gesture: it says, "Look, we are what we have always been, and you have not Englished us". That is of the greatest importance, and it is the one thing we owe MacDiarmid, without disbelief, without controversy, with a gratitude as simple as a glass of water. For the rest, his work stands like a warning: there are fanaticisms to come, pray thee avoid them. Or else as an encouragement to the discovery of new idioms, new ways in which to continue to tap the roots of our culture as best we can.

Allan Massie

THE ARTFUL ART OF
JAMES KENNAWAY

JAMES Kennaway died in 1968 at the age of forty. He had
published six novels, and left another, *Silence*,
uncompleted. (It has since appeared as a fragment.) All these
books are now being republished by Mainstream, a formidably
ambitious undertaking for a fledgling house, and one on which
they ought to be congratulated. In the tartan-lined bothy of
Scottish publishing the enterprise has a seriousness that is
wholly commendable.

The republication of the novels is testimony to the most
important fact about Kennaway, that he was a wholly
committed writer; by that I do not mean someone wedded to a
body of political dogma which he attempts to promote
through literature, but rather one devoted to the art of writing;
in his case to the art of writing fiction. The distinction is
important. There are those who see their novels primarily as a
means of expressing ideas — not necessarily a bad thing of
course, one can think without difficulty of worthwhile books
that fall into this category. Kennaway wasn't of this tendency
— I should be surprised to learn that what he thought about
anything was likely to be of much interest, the one exception to
this generalisation being his reflections on the problems of
writing fiction, and on the techniques by which these might be
at least circumvented. There can be no doubt as to his seriousness there. As he wrote to his mother, "it is becoming more and
more ludicrous to pretend that the point of my life is anything
other than writing . . . for days on end I'm totally immersed in
the work".

124

Nor is this republication the only sign of renewed interest in Kennaway. In January Jonathan Cape will be publishing a collection of notebooks and letters with a commentary by his wife, entitled *The Kennaway Papers*, while Mainstream have also commissioned Trevor Royle to write a biography.

It's clear, then, that Kennaway stocks are rising, and this at a point after his death when one might normally expect just the opposite to happen. (Where for instance did Dylan Thomas's reputation stand in 1965?) Indeed, it may well be that Kennaway is more highly thought of now than when he was writing — he began in competition, as it were, with regional and working-class novelists fashionable in the 'fifties and 'sixties, and it was perhaps only with his last two novels, *Some Gorgeous Accident* and *The Cost of Living Like This*, that he caught a contemporary mode. At any rate he has enjoyed that peculiar posthumous fate of becoming a writer with particular appeal to other writers. He is emerging into general consciousness as one of the most important novelists of the 'fifties and 'sixties.

It is not quite the case that this has been registered in Scotland, for reasons which are interesting and complex. In the first place he has been regarded as less than Scottish, partly because the time when he was writing saw the appearance of a number of very talented *authentically incontrovertibly* Scottish writers: Gordon Williams, Sharp, Hind, McIlvanney. The Great Scottish Novel (which has, of course, been written a good many times) seemed just round the corner. Kennaway hadn't entered that tournament; maybe he seemed a bit irrelevant, even though Francis Russell Hart in *The Scottish Novel* was to describe McIlvanney's *A Gift from Nessus* as "Kennaway's *Bells of Shoreditch* translated into a contemporary Glaswegian world".

One might dwell for a moment on this question of Scottishness, for it is a load many writers have to bear. We are always being tested — perhaps we also test ourselves — against our Scottishness. One may come to feel a sympathy for Graham Greene's expressed distaste for the label "a Catholic writer";

his preference for being seen rather as "a writer who happens to be a Catholic" also striking a responsive chord. Nevertheless, one cannot ignore the existence of those who insist on applying a test of Scottishness, even while one wonders at the value of a test that would exclude writers like Giles Gordon, Emma Tennant, even Muriel Spark, as well as Kennaway. Possibly it reaches its ultimate absurdity in Maurice Lindsay's observation that after *The Prime of Miss Jean Brodie* Muriel Spark's work adorns English rather than Scottish literature. Can we, one wonders, afford such generosity?

The doubts come from a certain lack of self-confidence understandable in a nation that always feels in danger of falling into the position of a client. Accordingly, anything not insistently Scottish is *ipso facto* un-Scottish. This is a dangerous limitation, almost a wilful act of self-denial; it reflects too an unattractive inverted snobbery, the feeling that only the working class remains truly indigenous, born and bred in the authentic native tradition. Their fate being, it would seem, to have no opportunity to escape Scotland (a view contradicted by the very considerable mobility of the Scottish working class), and to be unaffected by anything un-Scottish (a view which ignores what the American cinema has contributed to West of Scotland working-class culture), they are felt somehow or other (how is never of course exactly expressed) to be *truer*. It is of course a manifestation of the same sort of class-consciousness that sees working-class life as being closer to reality: by which is meant, well, you know, real reality. This is of course another meaningless opinion, since there is no means of measuring reality.

Moreover, the view that the working class, particularly the West of Scotland working class, incorporates the authentic Scottish tradition from which all other experience deviates, is historically false. Its central preoccupation, the religious division exemplified in the bitter animosity of Rangers and Celtic, is an alien import. What, after all, has historical Scotland to do with the obsessions of Orange Lodges, the wilful revival of old quarrels which were settled here in the sixteenth century?

Nevertheless, the view persists. No one would deny that this culture represents one strand in Scottish life (even the religious bigotry has, alas, become again genuinely Scottish — I am merely indicating how recently the roots were planted here, how irrelevant they are to the sort of Scottish experience that concerned Scott, Hogg and Stevenson). Out of this cultural environment moreover there has come writing of great vitality and worth in the last twenty-five years. And it is a world to which Kennaway did not belong. When he attempts to touch it, as in the character of Mozart Anderson, the referee in *The Cost of Living Like This*, he loses his certainty of touch and relapses into whimsy. Alexander Scott is right when he says that "his Glasgow characters are caricatures" and that "his lack of contact with the contemporary Scottish environment is all too evident".

Perhaps he was attracted to the character by the energy he discerned in Glasgow. It offered something he needed, and he was insufficiently concerned to evaluate it. Energy though is something Kennaway's central characters always have — he had a Stendhalian feeling for it. It is a quality lacking in much contemporary fiction, and its presence in Kennaway is one of his strengths. It is not necessarily a reflection on him, but perhaps on the society he was writing about, that the energy of Kennaway's characters is never directed outwards; it is almost never *for* anything. Unlike the Church of Scotland's, their bush burns and is consumed. You find the same sort of self-destructive vitality in Gordon Williams's characters. Where there is rage it is destructive, never transforming.

If in this respect Kennaway does actually have something in common with the West-coast writers, his upbringing and interests kept him safe from the trap that lurks, even now, before the writer who has emerged from the working class, or whose original material derives from working-class experience. Such a writer's problem is that everything in his life, the fact of becoming a writer most of all, separates him from his background. It is no use pretending that it doesn't. In becoming a writer he almost invariably becomes middle class

127

in lifestyle if not affections. So he can write about working-class experience as it is realised by the child and the adolescent, but when he writes about grown men they nearly always exist as seen from that angle. It is difficult to use his own adult experience satisfactorily. Accordingly he comes up against the question which all novelists try to dodge, pretending it is not really important: what am I going to write about? What is my subject matter?

Now one does not have to make any claims for the superiority of middle-class culture to working-class culture to see that this problem is posed rather more urgently and testingly for the writer whose background and original experience are working class. Writing is by definition a literate art; and the presence of books in the home, and sales of those newspapers and magazines that give attention to literature, indicate clearly enough that the middle class is still a good deal more sympathetic to literacy than the working class. (I am using these great terms loosely and freely, well aware that there is a huge indeterminate and ever-spreading area between them, possibly nowadays larger than either.) Faced with this problem it's no wonder that the best, most talented and honest, writers from this sort of background find it difficult to go on writing novels. It's not just the problem of dealing in adult fashion with a way of life which, seen from outside, appears to select as its highspots those moments of protracted adolescence, Friday night and Saturday afternoon; it's the difficulty the writer experiences in connecting with more serious aspects of a life he can now view only from outside, from the perspective of a changed consciousness. Possibly the most interesting recent feeling towards the right treatment was the last section of Alan Spence's *Its Colours They Are Fine*; but it was also clear enough there how the narrator was disengaging himself; indeed it was a very beautiful and effective realisation of the process.

Of course all writers are in a sense expatriates, from class or nation, if only because they reflect on, and make use of, experience which to others is simply the natural way of living.

The very act of trying to extract significance from the moment, to evaluate action and feeling, to give a shape to experience, necessarily separates you from the way most people live their lives. In the end all experience becomes material, may even be sought for that purpose and not for itself. Kennaway was evidently well aware of this; I shall be surprised if we don't come on much thinking around this subject in his *Papers*. It gave his writing a self-awareness that was almost embarrassingly self-conscious. He was almost too artful, the art too clearly discerned.

* * *

His original expatriation took a conventional form. He went to school at Glenalmond. The Scottish Public Schools get a bad press two ways, for they are seen as being not only socially divisive like their English equivalents, but also as a sort of English fifth column. They deny the oft-proclaimed democracy of Scottish educational tradition, a democracy not always so evident in reality, and they breed Anglo-Scots, encouraging the brightest of their pupils to look to Oxford and Cambridge and to regard Scottish universities as second-best. Having been educated myself at the same school as Kennaway, ten years later, I think this is true enough. It still seems to me inevitable, and therefore probably right, that it should be so. I had never any doubt in those days that my career would centre on London and I'm sure Kennaway didn't either. It was not just that London seemed to be where the action was (wasn't Kennaway right in that assumption in the 1950s?) it was also the inescapable consequence of political realities. A capital is the metropolis; its pull cannot be denied. Talent is naturally attracted there, because it cannot help feeling that only there can it prove itself against the best. That may seem harsh but there it is. Anyone staying in Scotland and not risking going out couldn't fail to have doubts that he just wasn't good enough for the big league. (Footballers, I am sure, feel the same way; even Celtic couldn't hold Kenny Dalglish.)

Kennaway went then to Oxford, after National Service in the Cameron Highlanders, where he was commissioned of course. It was an influential period; it was to give him his first novel, *Tunes of Glory*; and also an attitude to life. He remained very much a man who had held a commission in a Highland regiment, one who attacked life with a good deal of panache.

Tunes of Glory was an unusually accomplished first novel:

> There is a high wall that surrounds Campbell Barracks, and in the winter there is often a layer of crusted snow on top of it. No civilian rightly knows what happens behind that grey wall but everybody is always curious, and people were more than ever curious one January a year or two ago. . . .

That opening paragraph speaks for itself. It has a confidence and audacity that are rare. On the other hand, it is not at all literary — even from the beginning Kennaway showed an understanding of one problem that faces the serious contemporary novelist: how to find an audience in an age which is looking to other media — first the cinema, then the television — for its dreams and imaginative interpretation of experience. His response was to imitate the directness and economy of which they are capable, to write in clean, sharp strokes. There is an invitation here too — enter this exclusive club. He was making the same appeal to snobbery as sophisticated but less ambitious writers in a literary sense, like Fleming and Raven.

Tunes of Glory is dominated by the figure of Jock Sinclair, war hero, hard-drinking macho Scot, whose path to the acting colonelcy has been by way of Barlinnie Jail and the regimental band. Jock is a hero, but a very limited one; the time for his approach is past. Interestingly enough, Jock Sinclair is, in conception and treatment, very much a figure in a recognisable Scottish tradition — the hardman with hidden depths of sensibility which, without the aid of liquor, he cannot articulate. Then, he falls easily into tones of lachrymose sentimentality. "Women like you don't understand. You see us when we're drunk and playing the fool. You never know the real men. You don't see the other side. . . ." No wonder that in a minute "his eyes were brimming with a sort of hot pride". Then she (his actress mistress) was "hurt and he saw that he had hurt her. His own face screwed up in the same pain that he had inflicted . . .".

In one sense Jock is a modern Alan Breck (but without the complications of divided loyalties) from Stevenson's *Kidnapped*; he has lived for the love of glory, and he finds himself lost in a world where glory is no longer for the winning. He can momentarily recapture it and, with it, his magic for others; but he knows in his heart his time is past.

Opposed to him is the Staff College, Eton and Cambridge, product, Colonel Barrow. You could, somewhat fancifully, take the clash as representing the two sides of Kennaway: Scots background versus Oxford and London; in it Jock has all the energy. Barrow is disoriented. He doesn't belong. He has lost his wife, along with his past, and the conventional novelistic excuse that this is connected with his experience as a Jap POW doesn't account satisfactorily for his weakness. But in fact Barrow is the merest sketch for a character — he is good enough for John Mills to give substance to in the movie that was to be made. Kennaway's precocious technical skill and vivid visualising imagination were not matched by a mature sensibility. It is not really surprising that *Tunes of Glory* was a better film than it was a novel — you can't really read it now without seeing Guinness and Mills, and Susannah York muffled in a shawl, and Gordon Jackson, Dennis Price and Duncan Macrae. It was that sort of good bad book.

He followed it five years later — film scripts intervened and he was still working for Longman's on a part-time basis — with *Household Ghosts*, in the opinion of many his best book; it is also the only one of his four serious books to have a largely Scottish setting. It is too in a recognisably Scottish vein, reminiscent of the last (and best) novels of Eric Linklater in its concern for the working out of the influence of heredity — something which also marked it as a modern work, for this theme is only important in a society that feels disinherited.

But Kennaway's Angus gentry, Pink and Mary, are in a worse boat than that, for, like Linklater's narrator in *The House of Gair*, they are also cursed by such heredity as they are in fact aware of. So also is David Dow, the modernistic scientist (a cousin of theirs too) who challenges Mary, and is ready to rescue (or destroy) her. The pair of them re-enact another old Scottish drama — they are Knox and Mary Queen of Scots, the rational and romantic sides of Scottish history and character. That Knox is the one found wanting may be taken as evidence of how Kennaway is a modern writer: nothing is so discredited as reason.

More important from his own point of view Kennaway found here what was to be his characteristic method. Each novelist has that, the way in which he finds it possible to write a novel. For each writer the discovery is a voyage with its peculiar interest, which leads in time to a certain horror and disgust, as he learns the full extent of his own incapacity; the realisation comes, ironically, precisely through the slow mastering of one angle of approach, one way of writing that by its very singularity excludes the possibility of doing it another way; without, that is, making the sort of departure that is almost a new beginning. (What broke Hemingway as much as drink and the blows on the head was perhaps his under-standing of what he had done; which was to forge a style that could convey sensation perfectly, even complex sensations, but which was useless when he wanted to deal in reflection, as in *For Whom The Bell Tolls* and, even more, *Islands in the Stream*.)

Kennaway, with his cinematicising imagination and with a respect for the conventionally dramatic, found the structure of his method to be that old tried and trusted whore — the triangle. Usually it is two men and a girl (*Household Ghosts, Bells of Shoreditch, Some Gorgeous Accident*); in *The Cost of Living Like This*, a man and two girls. Either way he was able to put his characters in positions where intensity of emotion and keenness of sensation were dominant. His girls want their men; his men want their girls, but — Scottish enough this? — also want to be free of them. Everything turns and twists on this.

The man's masculinity requires him to receive love, but makes him reluctant to give it back.

These simple emotions gained from the sophisticated settings Kennaway found for them. The tearing loves of his characters are the more effectively rendered for being imprisoned in the bodies of merchant bankers, doctors, war photographers, a Cabinet Office economist. This is not just a form of snobbery (though there is some of that there); Kennaway is able to make us respond to the tensions set up between public and private persona. His characters have other lives in which they are important and powerful people, or highly respectable; lives from which passion pulls them away; which their imp of guilt or inherited desire for self-destruction is eager to tear apart. He understood what Elizabethan dramatists and Hollywood moguls always knew by instinct, that the private hell of the glamorous is more dramatic than the hell of the character who is the subject of nobody's dreams.

Kennaway had too the ability to be able to imagine his characters working. It is often complained that work is excluded from fiction, and no doubt one reason is that many novelists have little knowledge of other work, or of work of the type called responsible; but another reason is that, however fascinating it may be, work is rarely dramatic. It doesn't often fill our imaginations. And it doesn't appeal to the deepest elements in our nature. You can make a novel about a man seeking power through his work; you can make one about a man whose work is destroyed by his private life. But a novel simply about work is, like so many jobs, usually a bore.

All the same it's an advantage for a novelist to have some idea what his characters are doing when they are not in bed or in bars; and Kennaway had this. I doubt if Julian (the economist of *The Cost of Living Like This*) is a very accurate picture of a member of the Cabinet Office — would C. P. Snow have recognised him? That doesn't matter; the suggestion of his life in that world gave depth to the novel.

Still the triangle had its limitations, and I think Kennaway was feeling them by the time he started *Silence*. Principally it made it impossible for him to write a social novel, one that could really act as a critique of the way we live now. His characters have simply too few links to the outside world, though he scrupulously gave them pasts — the long conversations between Mozart Anderson and Julian's wife Christabel, all exist to give Julian a past. It's instructive here to compare Kennaway with a major novelist whose characters also break themselves on the rocks of passion, Ford Madox Ford. One can at once see the advantage Ford derived from the density of his novels, and how thin Kennaway's look in comparison. As a result he had to rest too much on his symbols; the cancer from which Julian is dying was simply too heavy a load to carry. At the same time, because the society in which his characters live is never fully realised, he falls back excessively on descriptive reminiscence; or allows one character who has no real part in the action (Mozart again) or, in *Some Gorgeous Accident*, an intrusive authorial voice, to take an explanatory role.

All this suggests to me that Kennaway was confronting — but hadn't solved — the central technical problem facing a novelist today, which is how to achieve a nineteenth-century density of texture without nineteenth-century proximity. The fact that Kennaway kept experimenting (within his chosen limitation of the triangle) is evidence of his awareness. One of the novelist's problems is that his art deals with individual people who are members of society; unless he has a picture of society, his characters are irrelevant or out of balance; but if they become simply social types, they are dead. One of Kennaway's strengths was his awareness that society was changing, that mores do not remain the same, that standards of judgement shift, yet that there must still be standards of judgement; and he knew too that we live in a peculiarly inchoate period, uncertain of itself and yet self-satisfied; a paradox which he could only reveal. He hadn't yet found a way of treating this that was wholly satisfying; perhaps there was too much meretricious glitter in his world, perhaps he was too impressed by his characters (Jock Sinclair and Link in

Some Gorgeous Accident and Julian are all accorded a respect which hardly seems earned, or is too easily earned — as if Kennaway fell half in love with his creations); nevertheless we haven't had many writers who have determinedly attacked our age in the same way, and who have searched so intelligently for a keen way of treating it.

He is a writer who still has a lot to say to us, who can excite us when reading, and from whom we can learn. That's quite a lot; and it's good to think that all the novels will soon be in print.

John Fowles

COLLECTOR'S ITEM

*T*HE *Collector* was far from the first fiction I attempted, but
none previous to it had satisfied me, and at least I had
enough sense to know that if the writer is not satisfied, no one
else will be. All through the 1950s I had struggled above all
with *The Magus*, and been defeated on almost every count. The
germ of the idea of *The Collector* had already been with me
some time when, late in 1960, I sat down to try to develop it.
The first draft came very quickly in a month, though it was still
to need a lot of work before it was fit for submission.

The first readers were my wife and an old friend, who clearly
did not like it, I think mainly because they saw no relation
between the book and the person they knew. But it was written
in part as an exercise, to prove to myself that I could write "at a
distance" from private self (failure to achieve that objectivity
was a main reason I had had such trouble with *The Magus*). At
the time I noted in a diary that I must make it coolly "exterior"
and "Platonic". I was very innocent then. I did know how
deeply pleasant creating a villain and killing off a heroine can
be — on paper, I hasten to add.

The "germ of the idea" was one that is universal among
adolescent males — and perhaps adolescent females as well —
as a daydream. It is of the isolating (not necessarily
imprisoning) situation — the event or accident that throws one
in intimate contact, at least of a conversational kind, with
someone one loves, but cannot ordinarily hope to be close to.
It is of course a stock-in-trade of the romantic novel, in the
form of the desert island castaways, the air-crash survivors, the

136

couple stuck in an elevator, and so on. But something drove me
to create a young man who would not merely dream of such a
situation happening by chance, but deliberately construct it—
so to speak, fix the machinery so that the elevator must stop
between floors.

Two events in my own life were important. One was going to
see a performance of Bartok's opera *Bluebeard's Castle*. Its
symbolism impressed itself deeply on my then very vaguely
conceived theme. The other was stumbling on an account of a
bizarre court-case — if memory serves, at Croydon, a suburb
of London. A young man had kidnapped a girl and held her
secretly in an Anderson shelter (the "family" air-raid shelters
built during World War II) at the end of a garden. The
kidnapper made his victim strip to her underclothes, but did
not molest her in any other way. He then ordered her to dig an
entirely pointless hole in the ground, as if her only hope of
escape was to tunnel through to Australia. In the end she
managed to slip a note out of her prison, and was rescued. I
was not the only writer to spot this newspaper item. Long after
The Collector came out someone sent me a copy of the French
novelist Simone Jacquemard's *Le Veilleur de Nuit* ("The
Night Watchman"). To my surprise she too had evidently read
the case; and based a story, closer to the real-life original than
mine, on it.

Though *The Collector* was well received in Britain, it was
generally seen as a psychological thriller. Not for the last time,
American critics understood rather better what I was really
after, which was much more a sociological, or even biological,
novel — that is, the problem of creating healthy social beings
in a species with such differing levels of education, intelligence, background and luck in the genetic lottery. Certainly all
the conventional moral blame here is on Clegg's side. But that
raises the question of free will, whether we are all at equal
liberty to be "good". Equally certainly all the moral virtue is
not on Miranda's side. The question I wanted to put is this.
Who is to blame for evil and violence in society: the under-
privileged who can know no better or the overprivileged who

see to it, either actively or through apathy, that the educational, social and judicial systems that suit *their* interests best are the only ones allowed? It is Clegg who assassinated the Kennedy brothers, and tried to kill Pope John Paul only very recently. Of course such men are monsters; but the purpose of this book was to suggest that it is not enough to condemn and punish monstrosity. It has also to be understood. Until it is, we shall as social beings remain the victims of the cruel necessity — monstrosity, if you like — of biological evolution, which is as indifferent as Clegg himself towards concepts like human equality and fellow-feeling.

I was once asked if I could name the real culprit in *The Collector*. I gave the same answer as I would if the question had been widened to name all that is wrong in human society. It is very simple: bad schools. There is only one antidote to the Clegg in our fundamental biological situation. I think we are no nearer supplying it now than when I sat down to write this black fable in 1960.

Christine Bold

TEN GALLON TRAUMA

> *"Would I might prison in my words*
> *And so hold by me all the year*
> *Some portion of the Wilderness*
> *Of freedom that I walk in here."*
> —Owen Wister, *Journal*, 1889

> *"Who owns all of space? Death."*
> —Ted Hughes, *Crow*, 1971

THE projection of the Far West of America as some synthesis of "The Lone Ranger", "Gunsmoke" and "The Virginian" is such a cliché today that the most desensitized television addict will dismiss the cardboard concept with a knowing smile. We may indulge in the weekly fantasy but we acknowledge that it is "not really like that". And yet, if the modern Wild West leaves me with any one predominant impression, it must be this very swaggering cowboy, these false-fronted buildings, that main street showdown. Or, less specifically, it must be the aura of costume, artifice, and barely controlled violence on which the small-screen Western thrives. Around the fuzzily defined area which we call "the West" there exists an invisible Midgard serpent which feeds on its own fictional creations, encircling a land in which artifice has become the basis of reality. This land is indeed some type of "middle earth" in which the inhabitants accept others' and their own inventions and build their lives on top of those layers.

The pattern is no recent phenomenon or product of the electronic age. "Going west" seems always to have involved a process of loss and profit, a deliberate inversion of the eastern order of existence. In reaching the western wildernesses a man could lose his name, his enemies, his debts, his life. Profit might take the shape of a new identity, financial success, community influence, mythic status. The movement, to the individual's advantage or disadvantage, was inevitable and the cumulative effect a reassertion of the same pattern whose echoes reverberate through the prairies, the high plains and the mountains to the present day. To describe the phenomenon is, of course, to simplify it, but it is true that, as a westward traveller, I have become more and more insistently aware of the westerners' need for accretion.

Owen Wister went west in 1885, discarding illness, moral uncertainty, East Coast inhibition and reaping health, adventure and fame in his major product of that experience — *The Virginian*. Wister's book exploded into public acclaim in 1902, the first truly heroic cowboy novel, which has since spawned countless imitations, sophistications and degradations of his basic mythic structure — including a distorted television adaptation which has foregrounded the title well into the present while submerging the author's identity and his original characterisation in near anonymity. But if the westernising process to which I have gestured is to be understood as both an individual and communal experience, Owen Wister remains one of the most fruitful means of access to the notion of self-imposed "cowboy-ism". He travelled west more than a dozen times in fifteen years, always returning to Philadelphia and always recording his impressions and reactions in the notebooks which accompanied him on each trip.

> 30th June, 1885. Now we've left the region of spitting chimneys and heaps of smouldering coal. . . . Those furnaces are hateful — they seemed like rows of grinning hellish mouths.

4th July, 1885. We're 8,200 feet up in the air, and it's cold. The air is better than all other air. Each breath you take tells you no one else has ever used it before you.

From Pennsylvania to Wyoming is from the poison of the man-made to the untouched and untamed elemental. The inference, present in every westward vision, is that to be in the West is to live close to unspoiled nature. One strips down to the basics and shuffles off the constraining layers of civilisation which are inevitable adjuncts to life in the East. Yet the man who wrote these words reveals his own westernisation, visually and ideologically, in a putting on, a voluntary donning of facade. Escaping from the personality that he was, he became immersed in a whole panoply of play-acting, dressing-up, cushioning of himself in romantic guise.

6th September, 1887. My trip is nearly done, & I am very sorry. . . . During the past two months I have been mistaken for—
1 an Englishman
2 a drummer
3 a bartender
4 a stage driver.
. . . But in another day or so I shall be back where nobody takes me for anyone but myself, and my period of entertainment will have ceased for a long while.

Owen Wister was an anglophile lawyer whose tendency towards statements such as "The deluge of immigrants is diluting our Anglo-Saxon race pretty fast — poisoning us, in fact" eventually goaded the Irish Freedom National Bureau of Information into an angry retaliation, entitled, *Owen Wister, Advocate of Racial Hatred. An Unpatriotic American Who Seeks To Destroy American Traditions.* Yet he was also a prime figure in the fostering of American tradition. His achievement — and responsibility — is typically eulogised by his daughter:

The Virginian himself is the progenitor of the cowboy as a folk figure. Because of him, little boys wear ten-gallon hats and carry toy pistols. This one novel set the tradition of the West permanently.

And Wister himself began to play some approximation of that part. Pausing in Chicago to shed "the garments of civilisation", more and more he took on himself what we now regard as the stereotyped cowboy trappings. The guns, boots and hat became necessary contributions to his western experience and in Yellowstone "we were much stared at. The spurs jingled over the boards to such an extent that I took them off in shame". His journeys to Wyoming carried him into wilderness camps with friends and Indian guides, his life metamorphosed into that of a latter-day frontiersman who shot goat and bear, avoided the beaten track and damned tourists for marring the sublimity of nature. It seemed impossible for him to survive in the Far West without the adoption of this rôle.

The frontier chameleon still reigns. For me as a non-American today, the western experience is most memorably a series of sporadic images. It is a solid, suburban citizen gleefully brandishing his father's notched six-shooter over the tea-table. It is lunching in a wood-panelled, chandeliered restaurant with a ranchman turned professor, who addresses the waitresses as "ma'am", wears cowboy gear, sideburns, slicked-back hair and tells me that *he* is the Virginian of the twentieth century. It is gaping at a twenty-thousand-strong rodeo crowd, or the eighty thousand humans milling around at the state fair, where for male and female the predominant dress is partly or wholly a composite of cowboy boots, jeans, shirt, vest and hat. It is hearing my escort scoff, "Drugstore cowboys". It is knowing that in his cupboards, too, lie a pair of pointed, scroll-stitched boots, a flowery, quilt-yoked shirt, a black leather vest and a hundred-dollar ten-gallon hat. The dress code persists, but without the pragmatic meaning, so that the insistence is on the purely visual and the result is the one-dimensional effect of the screen. The bandana tied flamboyantly around the neck of the sweating, overweight salesman relates to the practicalities of his life not at all. For the lean, toiling cowboy it was his only protection from the suffocating dust or the blinding snow of the trail drive.

More blatantly, entering the West is waking, bleary-eyed, in a Greyhound bus, to be stridently and unexpectedly confronted with a gargantuan plasticised fort. A twenty-foot tall Buffalo Bill stands guard to bid the traveller welcome while giant billboards shriek garishly that here survives the Wild West. As abruptly as it appears, the mirage is passed, its blues, reds and purples jarring nonsensically in the scrubby undulations of green grass and grey sagebrush. Man extends the artifice of guise from himself to the land. And the juxta-position of land and imposed adornment strikes me as equally insubstantial. There is the landscape, immense and everlasting. There is the ornament, so out of tune with the colours and shapes surrounding it that it perches on the land, neither blending with it nor borrowing from it any sense of solid permanence.

> 3rd July, 1885. The country we're going through now was made before the Good Lord discovered that variety is the spice of life. . . . I like this continual passing of green void, without any growing things higher than a tuft of grass.

This is Wister riding through the Nebraskan prairies, the same land from which Buffalo Bill's fort now emerges so dramatically. The traveller who goes west by rail today will miss Nebraska's contribution to land embellishment. For good reason — Amtrak schedules its western journey so that the train slips through this blot on the West's glorious escutcheon by night. Perpetual flatness, horizontal distance lacking the perspective of mountain or gorge does not contribute well to the scenic ride they advertise. Everyone knows that Nebraska, unembellished, is boring. The state's reply, the literal mark it has made on the landscape, is the creation of vertical grandiosity in horizontal space. It is well voiced that the West's great phallic symbol is the gun. Less widely known is the existence of a much more immediate, demanding symbol in the heart of the heart of America. A 400-foot high state capitol protrudes from the centre of Lincoln, the 1978 "all-American city", shrieking its self-assertive virility in shape, status and ornament. Atop the rocket-shaped structure poses the Sower, tossing his seed across the land and straddling a defiant red light which sends forth its blinking glare by night, insistently reminding ground and air traffic of Nebraska's existence. So potently blatant was the result that its ripple of appeal spread to inflame the imagination of one of Europe's greatest chauvinists — Hitler. He was so impressed that he decided to make this building, and its city, capital of America after his victory — situation, structure, symbolism were perfect.

However, it is not only the tourist trap or the architectural oddity which sits so precariously, as Wister saw:

> 5th July, 1887. How impertinent in this vast extent of earth do the little upstart board houses that cluster round a station appear!

There are much less strident methods of imprinting omnipotent humanity on the land. Further west, the ego is comfortably sustained by the twelve- and fourteen-thousand foot mountains in whose shadows men build. In Wyoming no building rises higher than eleven storeys and the traveller can assure himself that this is the *real* West, lying unchanged and untamed. The mark is nonetheless still attempted. Towns exist as right-angled grid constructs huddling in the midst of flowing, non-angular space. In retreating to the mountains my eye was inevitably drawn to the discoloured gaps which yawn eerily in the healthy lushness of pine forest. Great expanses of wood have been cut down by succeeding generations of settlers and the struggling land cannot produce new growth. So much earth bears the human mark. The land prior to the white invasion can be realised only by imaginatively obliterating telegraph poles, roads, crop layouts, the green swaths of irrigation systems. It is said that the Indian is privileged because the Great Spirit formed his skin after the colour of the earth — the plains were predominantly brown with sand, rock, grass, a brownness men seek to belie for it smacks too nearly of death. It is only by recognising that much of the landscape results from man's industry that one realises the layers that have been constructed between unfettered nature and the western terrain one sees.

Of course man fences, cuts and digs for practical reasons, but in those acts he also proclaims his mastery and moulding of the earth. Wister did not show his possessive hand until much later, twelve years into this century, when he bought his 160 acres, establishing his own ranch on his parcelled site. Yet there are still other means of bending the Wild West to one's will.

> 3rd November, 1892; February, 1893; 16th July, 1895. The day was fine, and from the top of the peaks I took a number of photographs with the codac.... Yet, even if these prove successes, I doubt extremely their conveying any but a false impression. The splendid distance, the amplitude of earth, the stately stretch of country — these are the signal points in what I saw.... I had no sense of any interruption — no trend of country looked as if it stopped anywhere. ... Wish I could find out all about it — and master it — theoretically.

While damning those who crudely enforced their way of life on the pure land, Wister, too, publicly displayed his ability to grasp and pigeon-hole this strange country. From the first his rôle was articulate recorder. His journal was ever between the spectator and the object. He distanced himself from western life, noting the peculiar, the unsophisticated — "We're stopping at a place which says: 'Commit no nusents in this barn. Hitch no horse hear'." — and even in the supposed moment of communion his recourse was to the written word — "Great God! I've just killed a bear & I'm writing this by his bloody carcase — 6.30 a.m." Indeed, his climactic achievement in *The Virginian* was the gathering of the West into one volume, the presentation of *his* West, sculpted and prettified, to an eastern audience. His implements were pen and camera but just as surely was he involved in a drive to imprison and dominate.

The unalloyed mystique of the West survives still in glorious exceptions — in the Grand Canyon, the Yellowstone falls, the Monument Valley which we do not see in John Ford's "Stagecoach". The unspoiled becomes a mecca to whose edges thousands troop every year, eager witnesses to the uncontrollable power of nature. What do they see, or where do they look? In large part, through the fractional eye of a camera or telescope. The Grand Canyon is the embodiment of the limitless, for the river which has slowly and indomitably carved out its mile-deep course continues to gradually bite and erode. Yet limits are perpetually created — those of a photograph, a cinematic presentation, a television screen. It is a visual limitation which corresponds exactly to the visual emphasis on costume, personal and architectural. Focus is paramount to photography and focus is central to the westerner's ideological battle with the land. Focus can exclude this limitless space surrounding man, to concentrate on details of town, dress, household appliance. In the midst of immensity the focus is on the minute. To build on the land is to establish the limits of one's perception and it is to cushion oneself against the raw power of the elemental.

Many emigrants travelling across the western wilderness in the nineteenth century disintegrated into madness and death, overcome by the very land they came west to exploit. And I have found that to try, even mentally, to immerse oneself in the vision of the land untamed is a frightening act. The realisation of the land behind the land, the awesomely beautiful barrenness and savagery lurking beneath the lush surface, is akin to the sense of skeleton. Man shies from the image of himself as a pale structure of bones, angle knit to angle, as a gaping skull, empty sockets and grinning jaws, and he pads his sense of mortality with flamboyant costumes and superfluous ornaments. To live in the West is to be surrounded continually by this skeletal fear as it is magnified over the hundreds of thousands of square miles which is the landscape. There is ever the sense of a powerful infrastructure which presses urgently against the inroads of humanity and against which the farmer, most obviously, spends his life doing battle. The result of almost a century's handiwork is a very bare containment. Hiding the individual's mortality in dress, our sense of our communal mortality, emphasised in the vastness of this enduring land, must be blunted with the architectural overlay — building structure, façade.

> 2nd July, 1885. One must come to the West to realize what one may have most probably believed all one's life long — that it is a very much bigger place than the East.

The land must always win. Where we can perceive the limits of our own bodies, assess and temporarily conquer the challenge, the western landscape has no visible limits. If Norman Mailer, in utter disorientation, scrambled with dimension and comparison to describe the Vehicle Assembly Building at Cape Kennedy — where "one was still inside a closed space" — how much further beyond the human's conceptual ability is the unending Wild West. In truth, such dimensions cannot and have not been tamed, by artist or labourer, and in all things the westerner continues to keep that one, very short step in front of his environment. Wherever I go in the land there is perpetual activity. Sprinklers gush out their sustenance to crops which the land does not accept with graceful fertility; giant black ants, on closer sight the apparatus which operates oil wells, dip with desperate monotony to suck from the earth its hidden riches for clamouring man; tractors and drills shore the ruined roads frantically against the fall and rise in a repetitive display of the human's stubborn pre-occupation with his house of cards. Without even the sea to map some boundary I can travel for days across a treeless, unending flatness or crawl, ant-like, over disintegrating mountain roads towards an ever-receding horizon, sensing uneasily that in my coupé and with my ice-box, the joke is still on me.

Yet it would seem that some can ride through the awesome space and win, always. With the help of technological achievement — in the shape of the gun — the Lone Ranger continues his fight against crime, Marshal Matt Dillon stands, broad-shouldered and impassive, against the glare of noon to cut down his next evil opponent, Shane rides off into the sunset to bring peaceful security to another band of struggling settlers. And the audience, as avid in the West as in Britain, fights with them. The television battle is invariably set in the past and Owen Wister believed that the wildness of the West ended in the nineteenth century with the coming of barbed wire, trucks, railways. Yet there is a continuing demand for costume and ritual, for a restricted panorama of two rocks and a stunted tree, where good always defeats the evil, the uncivilised. The modern westerner burrows more and more deeply into the one-dimensional victories of the television screen, vicariously scoring against the common enemy which is not, after all, another human, but which, despite his frenzied efforts to ignore it, slithers to the very windows of his safety, shifts creakingly under the cellar floor.

Giles Gordon

THE THREE FACES OF INDIA

June 1980.

"THE future of India — the next ten years or more — will depend on Sanjay. Not on Indira but on Sanjay," said the Indian businessman in a hotel room in Bombay at the end of May. Within a month Sanjay was dead.

Every remark made about India seems to be contradicted by the next remark. Nevertheless, an attempt at a few facts first: it is the largest democracy, and seventh largest country in the world. It has 1,260,000 square miles, about the size of Europe; and a coastline of 3,535 miles. The population is 650,000,000, greater than those of Europe, Australia and South America combined: no wonder it's classified as a sub-continent. A Dutchman I met remarked that the population was 630 million. I said I thought it was 650 million. "What?" he said. "It's grown by twenty million in the last few days? That's good going, even for Indians."

Not the least of the reasons why Mrs Gandhi was ousted from power in 1977 was because she and, especially, her younger son Sanjay (the most influential person in the country from 1975 to 1977 — and at the time not even a Member of Parliament — as well as from January this year until his death), had widely urged compulsory contraception and, in some cases, sterilisation as a way of controlling the population expansion. No people like to be restrained from breeding but to the Indian peasant the practice, or even suggestion, of enforced sterilisation is clearly a symbolic quasi-death. A

149

family of fifteen feels more secure and important, less vulnerable to the ravages of life than a family of twelve, although the smaller family could live more comfortably than the larger. Every Indian knows that there's not enough space or work or wealth or food for more people but why should he be the one to exercise self-restraint?

I spent seven weeks during April and May 1980 in the sweltering heat (the temperature often over 100 degrees fahrenheit) of India, and visited three of the four main cities which bestride the country like the points of a slightly cock-eyed compass: Delhi, the capital, to the north; Calcutta, which was the capital until the British decreed otherwise in 1911, to the east; and Bombay, whose harbour skyline astonishingly reminded me of New York's, to the west. Madras, the fourth city, is to the deep south.

Delhi has a population of five million, Bombay of six, and Calcutta of seven which makes it the biggest city in India and the second largest in the Commonwealth, though it is thought that in a few years its always increasing population will outnumber the diminishing one of London. If those three cities muster eighteen million people, that leaves a lot of Indians. Most are peasants living way below the poverty line in villages.

By road Delhi is 880 miles from Calcutta; Calcutta is 1,300 miles from Bombay; Bombay is 878 miles from Delhi. Madras is 1,535 miles from Delhi. The distances are such that the state-owned Indian Airways operate a network of internal flights which serve over seventy cities from the four major bases. Until recently the price of tickets was cheap, even for Indians who needed to use internal flights, but fuel prices are rendering it certain that fewer people will be able to afford to fly, and the Indian economy will suffer. It has to be said that whereas Air India, the international airline, is efficient and elegant, Indian Airways can be chaotic and rudimentary.

I flew from Heathrow to Delhi, my main expenditure. Once in India, and living more than adequately, you don't have to spend in excess of £4 or £5 per day, and that includes a decent night's lodging and three meals. My luggage was lost somewhere on the flight but, to my surprise, found the next day. "No luggage is lost in India," said an airline official, the first of hundreds of lies I heard uttered with confidence. A visit to the Aladdin's cave of lost luggage at Delhi Airport was sufficient to refute the statement. That's a minor instance but it seems that living in India makes it difficult for its denizens to distinguish fantasy from fact if not truth from fiction. Like the Irish — and unlike the Scots — they prefer to tell you what they think you'd prefer to hear.

In the capital I stayed at the Y.M.C.A. International Guest House, a stirring title for an efficient hotel in the centre of New Delhi. At the entrance a Sikh R.S.M.-figure, dressed in white pants and coat and vast turban surmounted by a huge red cockade, stood guard day and night. It took me two or three days to realise that there were three of him, on eight-hour shifts. He saluted when anyone entered. Very Raj, the whole establishment; as is Delhi, very establishment. The hotel had the best iced water I found in the country, a veritable nectar, probably the most essential single commodity in the summer months, especially with soft drinks — with which the Indians are obsessed — being stiff with sugar to the degree they are; and beer, when you can get it, nearly £1 a bottle. When Mrs Gandhi booted out non-Indian companies from the country, Coca-Cola was one to go. Overnight Campa-Cola was created, and to this day sometimes sold in Coca-Cola bottles with Coca-Cola tops. Gita Mehta's recent shrewd and abrasive book on marketing India to the West is called *Karma Cola* for obvious reasons.

At the Y.M.C.A. pots of tea were served in the afternoon by uniformed waiters. They varied the charge at whim. Some presented bills, others didn't, thinking they'd be paid more that way. They expected tips, and pursued non-tippers around the hotel. They'd do their damnedest not to serve them again. "I've no change," said an Australian. "I have change," said a waiter, an almost unique occurrence. Taxi drivers, shopkeepers and waiters in India make it a policy to say they've no change. That way they're more likely to gain notes than coins. A notice on the back of each bedroom door stated: "It is forbidden to tip the waiters. If anyone requests a tip please report them to the management in writing." It is typical of India to have such a notice and that no one should pay the slightest attention to it. Typical also that it should state "in writing". Everything has to be written if credence is to be paid to it, preferably in duplicate or triplicate.

Connaught Place, Delhi's main shopping centre, is faintly reminiscent of Eastbourne or Bognor Regis, England's faded Georgian seaside resorts. It is also said to be the centre of drug traffic in India and perhaps Asia. "Hello, friend," I was greeted many times. "Which country from?" "Scotland." Comment was rarely made upon learning my country of origin. The question is asked not out of interest in the answer — Scotland or the North Pole is all one to them — but as a conversational gambit. They follow relentlessly as you walk on. "You want best hash?" If you decline, they add "Very cheap", and if you still decline they say, incredulously: "Why not?" to which the only answer, which I became adept at offering, was: "I've got too much already". Immediately they melted away. No one asked me to sell though they invariably wanted to buy European goods — watches, pens, radios — or dollars or, even, sterling. They rarely had the currency when it came to the point.

Also in Connaught Place: "Hallo, friend. Which country from? You want girl? I take you lovely girl." I shook my head, walked on. "You want boy?" More head-shake. "You want animal then?" Only a touch of surprise in his voice. Not much in India is a joke.

A motorcycle-rickshaw driver told me that he had a cousin in Broughty Ferry, and (I couldn't follow the details) he sends him hashish through a diplomatic pouch. "Everyone in India has friends," he said, winking. We drove through the Lutyens government buildings set amidst the parched but serene lawns of New Delhi. They'd look more at home by the Thames and the Palace of Westminster would look less out of place next to the Red Fort or Humayun's Tomb or the Qutb Minar or any one of the mosques or temples of Delhi.

No wonder most Indians seem deeply confused and ambivalent about the British, and the influence of the British in India, perhaps more so in Delhi than in other places. The government buildings, neurotically poised between the European Renaissance and a more Oriental style, are a case in point. Is India looking west or east? It's a bewildering accident of history that English is the only common language between Indians from different parts of the country. He who speaks Hindi almost definitely won't speak Bengali or Urdu, so they converse in their versions of English. The way they use the Queen Empress's tongue is at least original, or was until Peter Sellers got to grips with it in the 'sixties. I often found it impossible, especially with tannoy announcements in railway stations or airports, to tell whether English or an Indian language was being spoken.

The British legacy (India became independent in 1947) is seen at its best in the network of roads and railways, although both will soon be in need of radical repairs and overhauling, which neither has had since Independence. The trains leave on time, even if they stop five minutes later. A less forgivable relic of our time there is in the aspirations of most poor Indians to become clerks, fillers-in of cash memos — as they call bills or receipts — and other meaningless scraps of paper. You even receive bills for ice creams, with the correct flavour ticked. No Indian trusts any other Indian, especially with money, therefore everything has to be written down innumerable times, and checked and counter-checked. Tens of millions must be kept in work this way, and accountants and auditors thrive. Trees don't. Indeed, there's a severe shortage but it isn't stopping the frenetic transposition of wood into paper for the most vacuous purposes. Carbon paper's in short supply, too. Nearly everything is copied by hand, which helps the days to pass more quickly even if it leads to a higher degree of error than otherwise would be the case.

There are more white cows and black bullocks in the streets

153

of Delhi (Calcutta has fewer and Bombay none) than in the fields of East Lothian. The sacred animals wander around doing traffic policemen out of work. If a bus driver inadvertently hits a cow both his passengers and passers-by will try to lynch him, and everyone resolves never to travel with that driver on that bus again. The driver is given another route, and the bus number plate is changed.

Which takes us to the heart of the matter, or at least away from the mind. Throughout the centuries, India's greatest influence on other countries and world thought has been spiritual. Today, approximately 85 per cent of the population is Hindu, 10 per cent Moslem, 2 per cent Christian, 1.7 per cent Sikh, 0.06 per cent Buddhist, 0.05 per cent Jain and 0.03 per cent Zoroastrian. In spite of the mass of gods and goddesses, incarnated and reincarnated in different shapes (my favourite is Ganesh, son of Siva and Parvati, who has an elephant's head, his own having been severed by his dad; he is the household god of prosperity), Hindus essentially believe in the oneness of the Supreme Being. Not only do they believe that their gods and goddesses are reincarnated but that they are too. Last time round, a man may have been an insect; next time he may be a bird. This life is just one of many to be borne with stoicism rather than fortitude, being but a stage on the path to nirvana. In practice in their everyday lives this leads to Hindus — and, by extension, Indians as the Hindu influence culturally and numerically is so persuasive — being apathetic. Or, as Gita Mehta puts it: "Being Hindu means never having to say you're sorry." The most characteristic gesture of an Indian is the shrug of the head, a more irritating because more pervasive gesture than the Gallic shrug of the shoulders. It indicates total resignation in the face of the slightest obstacle. If countries are granted or achieve religions that are appropriate to their physical conditions, Hinduism is the panacea for India. It makes it possible for the people to accept their impossible lives knowing that this is but one lifetime out of many. It also means that they're unlikely to fight against their misfortune. Many believe, and I'm of their number, that their acceptance of the tenets of Hinduism contributes to the low standard of living in the country.

The most obvious example of this is in the Indian's respect for animal life. Cows (and not just sacred ones) wander about the bazaars of city and village nibbling and stealing vegetables and fruit from baskets and stalls, and nothing much — only the odd "shoo" — is done to restrain them, even by shopkeepers. No one seems to mind that a cow may have first partaken of their mangoes or limes. Deer herds guzzle the growing sugar-cane. The destruction wrought on crops by the all-pervading monkeys and peacocks is colossal. And when there is famine or near famine, which is frequently, the peasant prefers to starve with his cattle than eat the beasts. Many people, and not only the elderly, spend hours each day in contemplation and prayer. In spite of the country's poverty, millions have utter contempt for money and do nothing to improve their conditions.

The streets of Delhi — and everywhere else — are awash with colour: the sarees of the women are more exotic than rainbows; and the usually white cotton and linen garments of the men provide a fastidious contrast. Many people live on the streets, having their beds there. The beggars tend to lie or crouch or crawl on the pavements and move into the gutters as darkness falls. What I hadn't anticipated was the range and ingenuity of the beggars' deformities. They leave the imaginings of Bosch and Peake at the starting post, let alone one's own preconceptions of them. It's appalling that one (and I know from talking to others that it's not only me) can be so sickened, devastated and humbled by the beggars — the beggars, quite apart from the poverty — when one first sets foot in the country yet within weeks, *because* their presence is so all-pervading and the horrors of peace so nightmarish, feel somewhat anaesthetised against their insistence and ubiquity.

Many are said to be extremely rich, and some leave fortunes when they die. Begging is their trade or profession. Hindus believe it is good to give alms, therefore many are seen to reward beggars even when not solicited. There is much competition among the alms seekers to be "good beggars",

155

which means to have injuries or afflictions which are likely to appal people to such a degree that they'll shower rupees upon them. It is said that beggars with, say, only a foot missing may pluck from a busy street a baby or young child, and break bones in the infant's body in such a grotesque way that those who see him or her thereafter will be moved to pity. The child will grow up to believe that his or her protector is a parent. The parents of the child will soon recover from the loss of their son or daughter as they will have quite a few other mouths to fill and bodies to clothe. All this is terrible, and hardened and immune though you become (for the sake of your own peace of mind) to hands being held out — if the beggar has hands — I suspect that the experience of beggars in Indian cities scars your retina for life.

Day and night in Calcutta naked babies lie — if they're lucky, on filthy sheets — on pavements and roads in the centre of the city, asleep or, if awake, crying. Sometimes their mothers are with them, more often not. Only very occasionally do you see a father around. The evening I arrived (you could have wrung the humidity out of the air) a beautiful young woman, her naked infant clinging to her front, accompanied me along the edge of the maidan — the two-mile by one-mile public park in the centre of Calcutta that acts as a poultice to the sore that is the city — for twenty minutes. It became a mental battle of wills. She must have known after a minute or two that I wouldn't give, and I wouldn't give later because I hadn't succumbed immediately.

One person I met, of Indian ancestry but from Guiana, took a beggar into a Calcutta restaurant and bought him a meal. The beggar ate mightily, the waiters were furious. Most people who eat in restaurants of the cities — as opposed to the innumerable cafés — are fat and over-fed. The difference between the rich and poor is far, far greater than, for instance, in the U.K.

When I arrived in Calcutta the proprietor of my exceedingly modest hotel (a magnificent elderly man with long white hair who was writing to Mrs Thatcher to complain about a well-to-do Indian civil servant having been convicted of shoplifting in Oxford Street) said: "Why do you come to this hell on earth?" He meant the city, not his hotel. Everywhere roof fans whirred and thrashed round day and night, and any garment that was washed was dry in twenty minutes. No one who can avoid it steps out of doors between the hours of 10.00 a.m. and 5.00 p.m. An ice cream man suggested I should have a drink instead as the ice cream would be dripping to the ground before I could get it near to my tongue.

Calcutta is straight out of Dickens, with heat and humidity in place of cold and smog. It's the only city in India where rickshaws are still pulled by hand, by men. A few years ago the rickshaw men voted overwhelmingly against transferring to bicycles, as in other cities, because they mostly couldn't afford the cost. It's disturbing seeing an interminable succession of skinny Indians pulling two fat people sitting in state. It's fashionable these days — thanks to sympathetic books by Geoffrey Moorhouse and others — to defend Calcutta, even eulogise it. As the indispensable *Fodor's Guide to India* puts it, it's a Manchester in the days before the welfare state began to blur the rough edges of the Industrial Revolution. It's Victorian in its outlook and its appearance: some of the grey, classical squares could be Glasgow. It's the essential industrial city of India, the engine-room of the country's economy.

It's not a place where you go sightseeing. Nevertheless, the Victoria Memorial, a monster wedding cake set on the green lawn of the maidan, is an unabashed shrine to 200 years of British rule. The Queen Empress (she even calls herself that in letters) is the star. She peers imperiously from plinths and canvases galore. Her Balmoral desk and piano are there to add to the nostalgia and authenticity. Portraits of every governor-general from Warren Hastings to Louis Mountbatten glower from the walls, and space has been made for two quite embarrassing paintings of the present occupant of Buckingham Palace and her consort. When I visited the Memorial it was crammed with Indian visitors of all ages, excitedly reading the captions. The collection of exquisite Mughal paintings in the same building was virtually ignored.

Outside I was accosted by a man wanting his two monkeys to dance for me. I declined the offer. "Are you French?" "No, Scots." "Very cheap for a Scotsman to have monkeys dance."

On Howrah Bridge, below which floods and seeps the wide Hooghly River, beggars sat and with amazing energy banged cymbals together, both to indicate a willingness to work and to proclaim that they're there. The bridge itself is a microcosm of Indian life, with people hurrying to and from Howrah railway station; on the platform of which families camp, their belongings heaped about them. Perhaps their trains are tomorrow, or the day after. . . .

I flew from Calcutta's Dum-Dum airport (where the bullets were made) to Bombay's Santa Cruz airport, though the coach ride to the centre of the city was so lengthy that I felt I'd been driven from Calcutta. Bombay lodges in the Arabian Sea — yearningly looking west — and is an island, a little apart from the mainland. In every other respect, it's far apart from the rest of India. It's a stylish city, a melting pot of cultures, architecture and others. The coach from the airport drove through slums and shanty dwellings, miles of them, as dilapidated and dehumanised as any I'd seen in India. Some of the rooftops were surmounted by huge airline advertisements urging the world to fly with them. The juxtaposition was utterly offensive. Maybe it was thought no one, eyes mesmerised by the sky, would observe the squalid dwellings and foul conditions below.

Bombay city proper is cleared of slums and designed as if it exists exclusively for international businessmen, travellers, playboys and Indians on the make — or, rather, who have made it. For the traveller, near to Bombay are the Ellora and Ajanta Caves, truly two of the wonders of the world. The Gateway of India at the harbour, built to commemorate George V's visit in 1911, is a sullen and arrogant chunk of red stone that is typical of the city's lack of indigenous, Indian character. The large Taj Mahal hotel by the Gateway is handsome and said to be the best — as well as the most expensive — in the country. The Arabs, with whom Bombay is stuffed, used to stay there but — to the relief of management and other guests — have largely moved to the new Sheraton. The white-garbed Arabs (the black-clothed women, bodies as well as faces hidden, seem to spend most of their time indoors) drift around the town, invariably dangling strings of beads from their fingers. Bombay is the most accessible city from the Gulf and they fly in hoping that their boredom may be alleviated by the fleshpots. They're not much liked; an economics lecturer whom I bought a drink after he had narrowly escaped being knocked down by a speeding car said: "We detest the Arabs but need their money."

Unlike any other Indian city, Bombay looks and feels international. It's expansively laid out with elegant modern buildings. Many more are going up. The coast and beaches and bays with their tropical vegetation, the winking neon signs and lights at night, the hotels along the seafront proclaim this as a city apart, so much so that people in search of better fortune pour into Bombay from all over India (as they used to go to London). They believe that anything is possible in Bombay, that their lives will inevitably be transformed.

Two people in search of work told me their life stories at some length. One was a lorry driver and chauffeur who had worked for a Plymouth Brethren family in Delhi and was sure there must be Plymouth Brethren in Bombay. There weren't, or if there were he failed to find them, and neither the Salvation Army nor Y.W.C.A. could help. His family were in Delhi, they didn't know he was out of work, could I give him a few rupees to enable him to get the bus back? The other was an agriculture graduate who had been told in the north that there were lots of jobs on the land being advertised in Bombay and filled from there. So there were, but every day when an advertisement appeared 200 people applied and those native to the area invariably landed it. He had no money to return to his village, and spent the long hours between interviews in the Prince of

Wales Museum. Both men volunteered that they would repay me the next time we met.

Elections to the Lower House took place in eight states, including Maharashtra, of which Bombay is the capital, as I was about to leave India. In Bombay as much canvassing went on as it does here. The two main parties, Congress and Janata, always have difficulty speculating who will win any election as 85 per cent of the population is still illiterate. If an election speech is made in a village or in a less sophisticated area of a city the people are likely thereafter to vote for the candidate or party which made the speech, believing implicitly all that's been said. There's consternation if both parties canvass, and people withhold their votes, knowing that someone hasn't been telling the whole truth. In Bombay alcohol wasn't served to Indians for five days before polling in case voters might have been induced to place their cross against the wrong name.

I shared a room in Bombay with three Indians, each in the city on business. One sold American trucks to Arabs. Each, clearly, was successful, agreeable and well informed. Each stated, and with some fervour, that their country was dangerously dependent on one man, Sanjay Gandhi. His mother was growing old, as her father Pandit Nehru was when still in power, as seems to happen to all leading politicians. Sanjay was groomed for succession by his mother, indeed he was the most powerful person in the country in all but title as his influence upon the Prime Minister was total.

I met many Indians of all kinds, castes, classes and occupations. They were without exception proud of their democracy and didn't regard the achievement and influence of Sanjay as in any way incompatible with their democracy, as much as anything for the pragmatic reason that there was no politician of equal charisma, stature, vision and drive. Gandhi, Nehru, Indira, Sanjay. That was the roll call. The question now is: will Mrs Gandhi have the strength, stamina, strength of character and personality to soldier on until a natural successor proclaims him- or herself? The answer is important to the entire world.

Peter Porter

CANZONE

What will I wish at my birthday?
    Only that after fifty-two years
        That the world should be
        As it is, but better—
I cannot imagine greater minds
        Than have already lived,
        Yet expect to be surprised
By new shreds of the immaculate,
        And I rejoice to know
        That the round arcanum
Welcoming all solvers of riddles
        Not open to me
        Will always be in place
Whoever the coming barbarians are
        Or those who learn to live
        In the dark of entropy,
And if the oracle, one of the fifty
        Amazing divinators,
        Speaks wittily, "You're
An analogue man, not a digital"
        I shall have nerve enough
        To reply to it
        That I intend to spin out
        Cautious connections
Whatever the fatigue of sense and syntax
        and not collapse in
Mystical muttering or nonsense of numbers.

161

Then those arrogants
Playing with Sudden Death
Or with slide projections of "Mise en Abyme"
May retire to their journals,
Savage importance
Pass over my head, it being no matter to me
That history's guest list
Has never included my name,
Nor that girls in production companies
Offering to show me New York
Remain just a dream—
I have no need to stand on the plates
Of the simulator
Of earthquakes,
I can shake in my shoes
Like that exaggerator John Donne,
Quivering in purest ego
Though bending none
To God or the ears of the saints,
Terrified beyond reason or resonance
And praying to find
Courage enough to say No
To strict Solons, absolutists enskied.
If the poet's cell
Have no magic, yet the poet's uncomfortable
Vision may form on the page:
Now the eel's trail ends
At a barrage across a stream,
Mist perennially drifting
Over the delta
To the twice enchanted emplacement
Where an egg of tyranny rocks
Ready in its nest.

Brian McCabe

THE BLIND

The blind old men who come arm-in-arm
on good-smelling days to the park—
they're grateful to the girl who brings them,
since it's seldom they have the chance
of a slow, recollective game of bowls.

The sunlight that signs their faces
with smudge-like marks where eyes were,
suggests to their memories a notion
of green, with summer all about.
Taking pleasure from the silence of grass
and the weight of the wood in the hand,
the old men are happy in the game
they play by sound intuition:

She is beautiful, young, sighted.
She stands at the far end of darkness,
clapping her small hands once, twice—
then he who's first to bowl stoops,
as if about to kneel and be blessed,
then throws. (They throw to the sound.)

As the black wood travels the green
she waits, motionless, and waits
as if by any slight impatience she might
alter the swing and slowing of the bowl.
When it's there she bows, she measures—
then calls the distance, the 'time':

'Seven feet, at four o'clock.' Or—
'Four inches, at six o'clock.'

And again she claps her hands.
Another player stoops, lets go . . .
This time it comes closer, and close enough
to enter the young girl's shadow.
When it kisses the jack, there's a *cloc*.
The old men smile.

George Mackay Brown

THE DAY OF THE OX

THERE are months and years when nothing happens. Nothing has happened here since I was a child, such as happened in the ancient stories of the coast.

There is always a time of full nets and empty nets.

There is a laden barn or an empty barn: the worm has been at the root, sun and rain have been at odds with the green shoots, the people have made a wrong dance at midsummer round the fire on the hill. Mostly, it is a barn half-way between plenty and dearth.

But a life-relish has gone out of the people. Why? We have been at peace for a generation. No ships have sailed from the Minch with a sharp gleam here and there, at prow or amidships.

The old burnt skulls knew such disturbances. Death sometimes made itself a feast in the village — old men and children, shepherd and fisherman and ploughman, knelt and fell before the knives of the southerners. Or, some winter, a fever burned them to the skull.

Yet we have their fine songs. The poet remembers a hundred rhymes and stories out of that hard time.

For thirty years there has been no new song on this quiet coast.

* * *

One evening, just before harvest, I went with others to the chief's house. He would tell us what things were to be done in the morning, if the weather was good — into what corner the first sickle must go, which women could be spared for gleaning and the binding of sheaves. The old man pointed at me — "You (he said) will put the sickle in first."

Heavy with all the suns of that good summer, I must have dropped into sleep where I sat among the harvesters.

I dreamed.

A man, a stranger, came into the chief's house. He said nothing. The chief's girl took a fish from the embers and offered it to the stranger, and a piece of bread. He took the food and ate it thanklessly beside the fire. Nor did he look any man or woman in the face. The girl had blown the hearth into flames. The man took off his coat, and his arm was golden-haired, as if it was circled by a harvest wind. And then he took off his woven hat, and a torrent of hair as bright as the sun fell over his shoulders.

The girl cried out with amazement.

Having eaten and licked his fingers, the man took his coat about him and left the hut, without a word or a sign of thanks. It was as if to him we were a company of shadows.

When I woke up, the people were sitting silently round the fire in the chief's house. Usually before we go to our separate huts, the poet tells an old story. Tonight, on the eve of harvest, the Song of Bread should have been on his tongue: an old blessing, first uttered on the coast a hundred years ago. But the poet was silent. At last he said, "I have had a bad dream. A man out of a time to come was here. He left a shadow in this house that will never go away. I am cold, I will say no more."

The girl said, "I have not seen a man so tall and bright and handsome. It was a dream. There are no such men in the world. I was glad to give him fish and bread in my dream."

Some of the other villagers said that they too had fallen asleep, and dreamed of an arrogant greedy sunlike stranger.

"I dreamed the same dream," said the chief. "I tell you this, it was a good dream, now on the eve of the harvest. Such brightness, such greed, such thanklessness. For so the elements work, in ways different from our ways. The earth takes our sweat and blood, and sometimes is generous to us, and sometimes is stingy. The sea, too, it covers the shore stones with twisting silver, or else it drowns a young man in his curragh and leaves the village hungry. That's the way of the elements. As for us, in our dream we dealt courteously with the stranger, and that is how it should be, as far as we understand things. . . . That golden thankless man, I tell you, is a good augury for the harvest."

* * *

Nothing happens along this coast. In the old days, after harvest, young men would go with knives into a boat and sail to some hidden island, where they were not known, and plunder, and come home again with pieces of silver, and blood on their daggers. But the last two generations have not known such adventure. The village has settled into a grey peace.

The dream that had come upon the village was whispered among the other villages of the coast. We suffered much mockery because of the dream. They laughed behind their hands. What kind of honey and heather ale had we drunk that night? How much extra malt had the brewing wife poured into the vat? Had there been many sore heads in our village the next morning?

"Let them mock on," said the chief. "The seagull has more understanding than them."

It seemed that the dream was a good augury. We reaped a bigger harvest than for many years.

In the time between equinox and solstice, there was no storm or rough winds on the sea. The fishing boats came to shore with torrents of living silver.

I think that that midwinter was the merriest time I had known in the village. Once or twice, the mouth of the poet trembled towards a new song, but nothing new came, only the old songs of snow and fire, darkness and drinking and dancing.

After that solstice, the chief became very bent and grey, as if a shadow had passed into him.

167

But he did not die.

Winter sifted into the hut of the blacksmith, and soaked into his flesh and gnawed at his marrow; and soon Blok was a burnt skull in the cairn. A child wept for Blok at the door of fire, the smithy, cold and silent now.

The snow of winter was at last only a streak or two on Kierfea across the Sound.

"It's time now," said the chief in his new grey voice, "to yoke the oxen."

It was time to yoke the first ox and unearth the plough from the summertime debris of the barn.

* * *

The monotony of another summer was about to begin. (And why had the vanished poet, who was a charred tongueless skull in the cave, why had he made such fine songs about plough and harrow, and the dialogue of seed and the ever-brightening sun, while our poet had nothing new to say about such things, but chanted over and over again the fire-forged and hammered words of the old poet, an old bright hoard?)

It was appointed to me, that spring, to open the door of the byre and to say to the ox, "Come, ox, it is time for us to work together, it is time to begin the ceremony of corn."

Then I had to loosen the ox from his ring at the wall, and to lead him forth into the light. He was so used, the ox, to the winter dark of the byre and the lantern twice a day, that his first sight of the sun put a kind of madness on him. He pranced, he smote the air with his hoof, his tail lashed, he put down his head as if he would charge at the horizon and break it! But soon, the yoke at his neck, he grew patient again, a friend to the village and the hungers of the village.

As I led the ox to the big field, followed by a crowd of villagers old and young, I saw the gulls rising from the crag in fierce broken circles. There had not been such rage and commotion among the cliff faces since the three whales had stranded there ten years ago.

I topped the ridge, gently urging the ox (and the cries of the villagers behind were almost a match for the blizzarding gulls).

Below me, on the shore, stood the winter stranger — the man in the dream — and a dozen others with him. Each man carried an axe. A ship like a great hollow bird was anchored in the Sound.

I pointed.

The villagers turned. Their mouths were suddenly silent, as they were gathered into a dream they would not wake from. They bowed their heads.

The strangers stood unmoving on the shore, among axe-glitterings.

The ox turned his horns from the sun towards the destroyers. He knelt, offering them his services.

Ron Butlin

JOURNAL OF A DEAD MAN

I AM called Samuel, but I am not a Jew. Would the Germans believe that? I am afraid of the Germans, they do terrible things my father told me about.

I am lying in bed when they come. They shine a torch into my eyes and say Jew, come with us. It is alright because I am not Jewish I say to them. I know that you have your orders but it is all a mistake. However, they make me get dressed and I give them cigarettes because they seem to be nice boys really, not yet twenty, and they don't know what it's all about.

Outside there is a lorry with "Juden" written on the side. The back of it is a cage, and there are Jews in it. It is not your fault, I say to the guards who sit with sten guns across their knees and look at me with their steady blue eyes. I am not Jewish, I say with a laugh, but that's not your fault you are not to know that. It will all be sorted out with your superiors when we arrive, I tell them. We are driven to an enormous building — that is, it feels enormous, I can't see it of course, because of the dark.

I climb out of the lorry and am taken down stairs at the side of the building. From there we go by lift through basements and sub-basements down many levels. The guards do not mistreat me as I expected they might, but when I stumble once or twice, then they hit me across the shoulders with the butts of their rifles; but it is not their fault, they think I am Jewish. Soon it will be sorted out and their chief will be giving me a drink upstairs in his office. He will apologise for the unfortunate error and inconvenience, saying that these things happen.

Then, as I expected, I am indeed called up to the Director's office and he apologises to me profusely. He shakes my hand cordially as we bid each other goodbye, and asks me if I would like to see how the Jews are looked after. I reply that it's alright, I know that the work has to be done and I am certain they do it well. Then his gentle German eyes gaze into mine, and he says that now I am here I must take the opportunity to see how it is done; then more firmly he says that it is really my duty to see that such work is carried out properly. He smiles: we go downstairs, he and I, in the company of two guards. On the way, he gives a descriptive tour of the building, and finally we arrive outside the room where he says "they" are kept.

When we walk in all the Jews flatten themselves against the walls and beg forgiveness. I whisper to one of them that I would like to forgive them and I don't want to hurt them really, but I am just there to watch by invitation of the Director; by forced invitation, I add with emphasis. The guards then bring some of them into a room like a hospital theatre and stick electrodes onto parts of their bodies. Then one of them switches on the current. I cannot look away because the Director is looking at me.

After two Jews have been dealt with like that, the switch is put into my hand and I am the one who must control the current. I know that it is not my fault because I am being forced to do it. Just before I turn on the current-switch, the Jew who is on the table asks my name, I do not want to say Samuel so I say Sam. Then he says. can't I hear the Lord calling me? I say nothing. The Director suggests that I make that Jew hear the word of the Lord, so I give him a blast of current and he writhes. Did you hear that? I say to him.

The Director comes up to me and says softly, it is a job that has to be done and you have proved yourself. He kisses me on both cheeks and there are tears of joy in my eyes.

* * *

When I was working in the supermarket yesterday, my wife came across some photographs of Ruth. They had been taken

171

at her flat one evening during dinner; as each course was served she had removed some of her clothing. My wife ripped up all the pictures. She told me that I was too old for that sort of thing, but I know that I am not too old to fall in love.

I do not love my wife. I do not even think of her very much, but I think of Ruth a lot though I know she cannot marry me. Sometimes in the evening when we are watching television, I look at my wife and think "you middle-aged bitch, you are fat and ugly and stupid, and I have nothing to say to you anymore, and you have nothing to say to me".

Then I think about Ruth. When I get into bed and make love to my wife, I try to remember all I can about Ruth until, for a few seconds, it is as if my wife becomes Ruth. But afterwards I am sad because I know that it was only my imagination.

Ruth is growing younger and more beautiful each year. She is becoming more intimate with me. Every time I recognise her I cut out her picture: I have many photographs of her now. Sometimes when my wife is out, I will close the curtains and switch on the small table-lamp, and then I will spread some of her pictures on the floor and gaze at them. Though she seems to be a different woman in each one, I recognise her for she is the woman I love when she leans back on a couch to pull on her stockings, and when she is sunbathing beside a deserted swimming-pool.

This evening I was looking at a photograph of her stepping out of a long white dress. She knows that her breasts are glorious because I have often told her so, and she touched them then while her eyes met mine. I looked very closely until once again I felt the caress of her fingertips and her tongue, and breathed in her scent, and felt the silk and lace against my skin. I gazed at her photograph until I knew she was there and heard her calling my name. Then I looked across the room to where she was stepping out of her long silk dress, and then once more she came towards me out of the darkness.

* * *

Every time I am taken into the basement by the Germans, I am not really very afraid because I know that it will always work out in the end. I know that although I will be forced to work the machine, the Germans will be my friends afterwards. But each time it happens they take longer and longer to believe that I am not a Jew, and in order to prove it I must do more and more work with the machine "to make them hear the word of God" as the Director says.

I cannot tell one Jew from another, so really I am dealing with the same Jew each time. And the Germans really all look the same except for the Director who wears a suit whereas the rest of them are in uniform. One night, however, a Jewess is brought in, and she is beautiful. The Director asks me if I want to have her before she goes on the machine. He says that at this moment she will be at her best, and also that she will do anything in the hope of release. I guess that this is one last trick of his to make me betray my suspected Jewishness and so I say yes, thinking that I will show him once and for all. Well, he says, she's all yours now.

She is standing rigid with fear and then, as I approach her, she spits at me. I get two of the Germans to take an arm each and hold her against the wall. She starts swearing at me and calling me a pig, and asking how could I, a Jew like herself, be here with these Germans and do this to her? I tell her that I am no Jew but she calls me a liar. I am standing only a few inches from her now and she is turning her face this way and that and screaming that I am a Jew and so to shut her up I grab her by the hair and kiss her on the mouth.

She tries to bite me but I am too quick for her and step back a pace. She is wearing a kind of hospital gown which is very unbecoming and so taking it in both hands I rip it open, and now I can see how beautiful she is! Behind me, the Germans are shouting encouragement, giving catcalls, whistling and clapping their hands. One of the guards holding her says in a low voice that it will go much easier for her if she doesn't struggle so much, she's going to get it anyway so she might as well relax and enjoy it. The other one, however, says that as she's going to get it anyway she may as well struggle if she wants.

173

As she raises her eyes to meet mine I see for the first time that it is Ruth. The shouting and the hand-clapping seem to be coming from further and further in the distance. She looks at me and says nothing. She and I are standing in total silence and then, out of the corner of my eye, I notice that though the guards still seem to hold her, this is an illusion; for I see that really it is as if the soldiers are painted onto the wall, and only by some sleight or trick of line do they appear to hold Ruth there.

Effortlessly then, Ruth places her hands on my shoulders and turns me round. Immediately I see that the Director and the guards are also painted; they are cut-outs that are ageing visibly and turning yellow even as I stand here. The basement is becoming very dirty and the walls are silently cracking apart. Ruth kisses me. The ceiling is disintegrating and I watch as unfamiliar stars drift slowly across the night sky.

My hand that is caressing her breast is trembling and becoming wrinkled. My breath is becoming more and more strained with effort. I must make love to her, she says. Her voice and caresses encourage me urgently. Above me now the stars are whirling dizzily. The walls have disappeared. Every kiss and every caress is an effort for me. She is holding me so tight and I am becoming frailer and frailer. I must make love to her she says, and I am certain that I am dying.

And then I see in her eyes that I must die and she has known this from the very beginning. I know now that I must make love to her and in the certainty of this I begin to climax and to die. Even as I do so the stars begin to slow down, and I am an old man recognising for the first time her love for me shining in her eyes as darkness comes over me, and bliss.

* * *

I had a dream last night: I was working in the store as usual and every woman there was Ruth. She was sitting on the counter and she was leaning against the shelves, and each one was gazing lovingly at me. Then she turned round from the end of one of the aisles and began walking towards me. As she approached she began undoing her blouse. Behind her I saw the manager come out of his office, it was the Director and he smiled at me. I heard laughter outside and saw the German guards were crowded at the shop window pressing their faces against the glass. But Ruth seemed unaware of all these people, she kept walking towards me and discarding her clothes. I tried to warn her but I couldn't speak and I was unable to move.

When she saw that I did not respond to her, she looked very hurt. Then she began to let her hands run gently over her body, they caressed her breasts and stroked between her thighs, and all the while the guards cheered loudly. I watched in horror and could do nothing. She became more and more excited and the cheering of the guards outside grew louder and louder as more and more of them pressed against the glass. Her breathing became quickened. The Director was standing beside me and gave me a conspiratorial wink. All at once I was able to speak and just as I shouted to her, the glass in the window gave way and the store was filled with Germans.

* * *

Always she comes to me out of the darkness, and afterwards she returns there. I switch off the table-lamp, open the curtains and finally I put away the pictures without looking at them again. My hand is shaking and often I feel very sad because I love her. I love her so much and I am with her for only so few moments at a time. For the rest it is days and years spent alone, time I cannot share with her.

My wife does not know what love is, or she has forgotten. And even when I am in the basement with the Germans and being made to work the machine, I have not forgotten Ruth — for at that moment I long for her so much that afterwards the guards sometimes have to unclasp my hand, finger by finger, from the switch.

* * *

This morning I rose from the dead. It is a time to perform miracles. My wife had betrayed me to the Germans saying that I was a Jew and a degenerate, and I looked at dirty pictures.

They came for me last night, took me in the lorry and down into the basement. They tied me to the table and turned on the machine.

But now I have risen from the dead. My wife is lying on the couch watching television. She has destroyed all the pictures of Ruth so as to keep us apart.

Ruth is not dead, she cannot die because she is younger and more beautiful each time she comes to me. But she is trapped in the darkness and I am trapped here.

My wife has forced us apart, but now she must bring us together. It is a time for miracles. She must dress as Ruth dresses that her body will grow younger and more beautiful.

She is dying and Ruth is coming towards her out of the darkness. Her body will be draped in silk and lace, and Ruth will gaze lovingly at me through her eyes.

We will be together for all time, because we who have risen from the dead become younger each day and never die.

The Germans are dead, my wife is dead, everyone is dead who has not been on the machine.

There are wounds on our hands and feet made by the machine, and it is by these that we recognise those whom we love and who will live forever.

Jack Debney

THE CROCODILE'S HEAD

I T was time, he thought, that he wrote his memoirs. It had long been his intention to do so but now he felt the moment to be right at last. "Got to set the record straight," he said out loud, not quite sure what he meant.

He found some paper and sat down at his desk. On the first sheet he wrote: *Algernon Hussein Abdel Salaam: a Life.* He studied this for a while then, dissatisfied, crossed it out. On the next sheet he wrote: *The Life of Algernon Hussein Abdel Salaam of Alexandria.* This suited him better. But how to begin? He pondered as he lit a Belmont.

He was a tall, thin, stooped man of fifty-five, who looked ten years older. The day before, Wednesday the 12th of May, 1965, his young wife had left him, after a period of increasing estrangement.

The Life of. . . . Not bad, he thought. He saw himself writing into the night, the light of the desk lamp shutting everything else out except his work, his pen moving over the pages. It was a vision which warmed him.

He decided to begin with yesterday's events. "My wife has decamped." No, that wasn't right. He wanted to start with a flourish — something that would express sorrow and yet courage too, a determination to go on whatever fate threw against him.

"Man, the crown of creation," he began, "is a foolish but stubborn being. Intended for greatness, he . . ."

He looked at what he'd just written. "Ballocks to that!" he said and fumbled in the packet for another cigarette.

* * *

He was on the balcony of the dar, their big house at the ezbah, with his morabia, his nanny. He was about eight, he estimated. He had just ordered the morabia to set up his woollen animals against the wall at the end. He was throwing a ball against them and knocking them over.

And beyond the curtain, in the upper room, his parents were quarrelling. He knew the quarrel was about Miss Colquhoun, his governess, and this dismayed him. For his parents to row was normal, as normal as it was for Miss Colquhoun to lead him away, out of the sound. She was always there at the right time, prematurely faded, young-old Miss Ursula Colquhoun with the sudden broad smile that took the tiredness from her face for a while, and the grey-blue eyes that gazed at him with such an amused and wistful affection, totally unlike the morabia's fawning, suffocating devotion. He liked making himself charming for Miss Colquhoun. The best thing in life for him then was when, after such a performance, she would stroke him on the head, smile, and say in mock-exasperation: "Oh Algernon, Algernon!"

Later that evening, hours after he'd been told to go to bed, he crept out onto the balcony and secretly watched the decrepit old gharry come slowly into the yard below. He saw Miss Colquhoun leave the house and seat herself in the gharry and watched the ghaffir load her cases and then get up beside the driver.

Miss Colquhoun had done something wrong, something to do with his father, he didn't understand what, but nothing, he knew, deserved sending her away. The ache in his throat spread and almost choked him.

The gharry left the yard and drove past the ezbah towards Mehalla where there was a station and where the ghaffir would wait with Miss Colquhoun for the next Alexandria train. He would put her on it and then come back to the dar.

Algernon observed the lights in the fields, where some of the peasants were sitting all night guarding the cotton against thieves. He tried to map out by the pinpoints of light where all his family's land lay, and he thought — when my parents are dead I'll have all this then. But what he meant, and hadn't words for, was that he'd search out Miss Colquhoun wherever she was and bring her back here, install her forever at the dar.

He heard some of the fellaheen laughing and talking to each other and then one fired a gun into the air and pretended there was a marauder. He listened to them playing and laughed silently to himself, a little soothed.

* * *

'Some months ago," he wrote, "I was walking along a narrow street in Manchela, not far from Mohamed Ali Square. I had a toothache and, prior to making an appointment with my dentist, I wondered whether I could find some tooth-tincture to relieve the pain. And then I saw before me, almost providentially it seems to me now, a chemist's."

Algernon Hussein went on to describe how he'd gone into the shop and had been much taken by the assistant, her prettiness, innocence and vivacity. This was the beginning of the chapter on his courtship and marriage which he knew wasn't going to be easy to write.

He struck up an acquaintanceship with the girl whose name was Amira. She was poor, badly educated, thoroughly ballardi, vulgar, but in spite of all this he had high hopes of her. Over the next few weeks he called in at the chemist's several times, on one pretext or another, making use of the opportunity to ask her questions about herself, her family, gradually building up a picture of her. She answered readily, seeming pleased to talk to him.

He thought long and seriously about Amira and then entered into negotiations with her father, who was interested but puzzled. He asked whether Algernon were Moslem or Nasrani. Algernon replied that he came from an old, well-established Moslem family, mentioned the money he'd received from the Government as compensation for land taken away from him because of the land reform, and talked vaguely but impressively about his "business interests".

"Your Arabic is a bit strange," Amira's father, Abdullah, said. "Are you an Englishman?"

Algernon explained that his mother had been English and his father Egyptian, and that he had lived for a long time after the war in England. He had married there, had children, and later divorced. He added that he held a British passport.

"Are you going back to England?"

"No," Algernon replied, "not now — I shall stay the rest of my life in Egypt. It's my country too, you know."

Abdullah laughed, somewhat mockingly. Then he paused for thought.

"My daughter's only sixteen," he said eventually. "The legal minimum age for a girl to marry, it's true, but she's much too young for you."

Algernon had prepared a speech on the advantages of marriage to older men and, without much hope, was just about to begin it when Abdullah went on, "It's also true that she needs someone with experience to guide her. Someone to keep her under control, eh?" Algernon Hussein smiled, trying to restrain the elation that was beginning now to replace his gloom. He knew that Abdullah had given his consent after all, and that only the details needed to be settled.

Pausing in his writing, Algernon thought of the humiliations of the wedding night, his naked sunken body as he walked towards the bed and Amira's shocked, frightened face staring at him from the pillow. In the bed he embraced her clumsily but as strongly as he could, trying to bring his tired flesh to life. But nothing happened. And, after a while, Amira moved out from under him and went across to the door. Her stocky, dark-brown body, with its over-plump haunches and short legs, became suddenly endearing to him. His penis began to stiffen at last and he thought to call her back to him. But she'd left the room; he didn't say anything and his penis slackened again.

After seven nights of sleeping in the spare room, Amira

allowed him to take her again to what was supposed to be their bed and, a passive sacrifice, she endured while he tried to work up enough desire for her to keep away the weakness and weariness he felt. Towards dawn he managed to penetrate her. It was a feeble spasm but it was done and she was no longer a virgin. She cried a little with the pain and the blood and then fell asleep beside him, her head on his shoulder, her thick sturdy arm across his chest — her first act of tenderness in their marriage and practically the last.

A little less than a month afterwards Amira told him, "I've got a job as a hostess at La Perle d'Orient."

"You've no need to work," he said. "And certainly not as a hostess."

"But I want to work. I'm so bored here. And I've been offered this job."

He knew from the stubborn set of her face and the irritable voice that it was useless to try to stop her. And for a time he chose to believe that she was just someone to dance with the customers and persuade them to buy expensive drinks. But he was forced to face the truth when, one afternoon, he arrived home earlier than he'd said and found Amira in their bed with an English sailor. It was the first time, so far as he knew, that she'd brought a customer to the flat.

The English sailor, disturbed in his love-making, jumped off the bed and struggled frantically into his clothes. Algernon watched, not sure how to react, whilst Amira, defiant, screamed abuse at him. Then, leaving the sailor to do up his trousers, he went away down the corridor to make himself some tea. He lingered there but had the bad luck to see Amira's client again — almost colliding with him in the corridor as he was trying to make a quiet departure.

The big, red-faced Englishman looked at him compassionately and then, his hand on the door knob, said, "Bad luck, mate."

Algernon Hussein the autobiographer, at his desk before the mound of white paper, tried to imitate the sailor's cockney accent.

"Baird luck, mite," he said in a falsely deep, stentorian voice and laughed.

* * *

He was sitting in Kerpy's bar. He had been writing his memoirs for most of the day and was tired but satisfied with what he'd done. He added a drop more water to his ouzo and toyed with a plate of mazairthes. It was time to go. Looking around for the waiter he saw Amira instead. She was just coming in with two men. They looked like Greeks, he thought.

The band had started playing again and Amira and one of her escorts went onto the narrow dance floor. Algernon, sitting against the window, in the dark rind of the dim light, hoped he'd be unnoticed.

He watched her attempting to dance — the vital but clumsy body in its garish yellow dress trying unsuccessfully to imitate the Greek's graceful steps. Algernon rose to attract the attention of the waiter. He had to get out quickly. And it was then that she saw him. She stopped dancing, saying something to the Greek who nodded and went over to join his companion at the bar.

Amira came and sat down at Algernon's table. She smiled at him and he smiled in return, but cautiously. She'd not been in touch with him at all for two months. For a while they said very little, shy with each other. But Algernon noted that he felt no hostility to her and she showed none of her customary contempt for him.

He didn't ask her where she was living but instead whether she was still working at La Perle d'Orient. She shrugged her shoulders. "Sometimes." Then she told him about the other clubs along the Corniche that she worked in; he could see that she had become a real professional, knowledgeable about the best terrain for her work, cynical about her customers. And he was amazed that none of this hurt him. In fact, he began to like Amira by him, her bright, hard tales.

They had some more ouzo, and then more.

Algernon Hussein brought the words through his drunkenness, enunciating extra clearly so that she couldn't possibly misunderstand him. "Why don't you come back to me, Amira?"

She looked surprised, then shook her head. But a few moments afterwards she asked, "What about my work?"

"You can continue going to the clubs, and otherwise use our flat. If you wish." He stroked her arm. "Ya helwa! Beautiful one!" he said. The maudlin tears filled his eyes.

Soon the two Greeks came to claim Amira. At Algernon's invitation they sat down, had a drink and then left with her. "She's hot stuff, boys!" Algernon roared after them, enjoying their embarrassed but conniving smiles, and the shocked disgusted looks of the other customers nearby. "Best bit of cunt in Alexandria!"

"Tomorrow," Amira said at parting. "I'll come back to you tomorrow."

Later, nearing his home in Mazaritah, Algernon noticed that the Nubian goods shop was still open. He wandered in and found himself looking at a crocodile's head. It smiled at him, in a rather tight-lipped way, and Algernon passed his hand along the line of the jaw. It fascinated him and he thought that Amira would find it amusing. So he bought the crocodile's head, stuffed it under his arm, and went home.

When he was in the flat he thought that the head seemed dustier and grubbier than in the shop, and that it wouldn't do any harm to put it into a bucket of water. This he did and then placed the bucket on the balcony outside his bedroom.

* * *

Next morning he awoke with a bad hangover. He stayed in most of the day, just going out briefly in late morning to buy flowers, chocolates, food and some wine.

Just before eight in the evening the bell rang. Amira was there, with a short, jowly, thick-set man.

"Ahlan, ya ostaa!" he said. "Going to let us in?"

Amira looked out of sorts, but nevertheless touched Algernon reassuringly on the cheek.

"He's from Damanhour. He's got to go back on the train tonight."

As though that explained and justified everything! Algernon felt vexed but said nothing. He stood aside to let them pass.

"It won't be for long," Amira said, and led the Damanhouri down the corridor to the bedroom.

"Get some beer ready for us, uncle!" the man called back.

"He'll get it if and when he chooses to get it!" Amira snapped and closed the bedroom door impatiently.

Algernon heard the shutters being opened, and then suddenly there was an appalling scream. He jumped up, terrified, and rushed into the bedroom. Amira was standing by the window whilst the Damanhouri was lying stretched out on the bed bawling with laughter. Algernon looked over Amira's shoulder. He saw the crocodile's head staring up at him from the bucket. He'd forgotten all about it! Its jaws had slackened with the water and now smiled at him widely and genially. But out of its mouth, between the borders of the smile, had crawled trails of bugs of various kinds. Some had fallen in the water, struggled and died there whilst the more astute ones had climbed to drier, safer ground on top of the half-floating head, where they still survived.

"It was a present," Algernon began lamely.

"A present!" Amira shouted. "Are you an idiot after all? What kind of present is that? You put the horrible thing there just to scare me, make fun of me!"

"No, Amira, listen — it wasn't like that at all. I was coming home last night and . . ."

"Get out!" She turned back to the bed and started undressing. "Get out, I said!"

Algernon left the door open. The Damanhouri's voice followed him down the corridor. "Hey, abu labban! Come back and close the door!"

"No!" Amira commanded. "Leave it as it is!"

Algernon Hussein sat down at his desk and looked at the pile of manuscript that lay there. He heard the bed begin to jingle and the Damanhouri grunting, Amira squealing theatrically. He drew a line under his last completed chapter and began to write.

"The land is dull sometimes — flatness, cotton fields, maize fields, canals, dykes. And then, the dar is dilapidated. The porch is rickety and the hand-rail on the roof is downright dangerous — just crumbling away. The whole place needs a lot of work done to it. We can manage, of course. But it'll take time and a lot of patience."

Bed-springs, bed-springs — how they rattled and screeched now! He looked over what he had just written. You're mad, Algernon, he thought, quite mad. We don't own the dar any more, let alone the land. It's all gone, all past.

But he went on writing.

"One night, we crept onto the balcony and watched the gharry being driven up below, do you remember, Amira? And the ghaffir piled their cases on it. Then we saw my father and mother come out of the house, get into the gharry and drive away to Mehalla, so they could catch the next Alexandria train.

"We watched the lights in the fields — some of the fellaheen were staying out all night to guard the cotton crop. And then we heard a gunshot. A fellah was pretending that there was a thief, making a game of it. Some of the other peasants began laughing and joking too, do you remember, Amira, my princess, do you really remember now? We laughed too and then went back into the bedroom, and how we laughed, not at the peasants any more, but because the house was ours now and all the land around, you couldn't walk it in a day, and the things we planned to do, it was all ours, O Amira, my princess! How we laughed and sang, the joy, and what we would do, so much strength, nothing would stop us, O Amira, princess, princess, how we laughed with the joy of it all!"

Algernon Hussein Abdel Salaam looked at what he had just written and suddenly, leaving a couple of inches of space, he wrote underneath, in vague, excited hope: "I am sad but free."

And, long after the Damanhouri had wished him a raucous goodbye, long after Amira had gone into the bathroom for a shower, he sat there, at his desk, within the circle of lamplight, trying to puzzle out what the sentence meant.

Jonathan Steffen

MAIDENHEAD AND MANHEAD

DEAR Tom,
Permit me at this juncture to remind you that, whatever the writers of lukewarm pornography might attempt to suggest to the contrary, there is in fact little or no similarity between the female pudendum and the verdant moss with which it is so frequently compared, *viz.* "the luxuriant moss of her pubes". Any close inspection of the two will reveal a number of fundamental differences. In the winter months the most conspicuous distinguishing features of moss are its greenness and its coldness: the pudendum is subject to no such climatic changes, and is entirely different in colour. In the summer months, and particularly after the application of weedkiller (which produces its optimum results during this warmer period) moss becomes brown, dry and crumbly: the Mount of Venus, whilst susceptible to charges of brownness and even of dryness, can never rightly be accused of being crumbly. Moreover, moss, be it soaked or shrivelled, is in no way as sexually arousing as the privy parts of the female: were it so, gardening would be a more popular profession, and I speak as one who has gardened professionally. The analogy is inexact.

I could continue in the same vein, and discuss melons. To me, the melon is a large, firm and heavy fruit, readily obtainable at most greengrocers and supermarkets. The differences between this and the female breast become immediately apparent, as any frustrated adolescent with a High Street round the corner will tell you. Further evidence for identification of the melon may be sought in the sticky labels which are often attached to their (frequently bumpy) skins; and I have no doubt that a comparison by weight of the melon and the mammary gland would produce grounds for differentiation equally conclusive. Shall I go on? Shall I analyse the strawberry, the sad lemon, the luscious peach and the unfortunate potato-sack? Is it really necessary for me to characterise the fig? No. And no again. The superimposition of the basic tendencies of the vegetable kingdom onto the unwavering factuality of the female body is false, mystifying and, frankly, boring. I have no words for the banana.

Her breasts.

Her breasts her breasts her breasts her breasts her breasts mean nothing if I say it like this — they become a sound, a typewriter-rhythm, a sequence of letters. Then how am I to speak of them? They were not ripe. They were not firm. They were not full. Not jelly on a plate, not pink blancmanges. Still less suspended teardrops or the trembling upturned chests of frightened sparrows. They have no correspondent in the phenomenal world to which I might refer in order to explain them. They were like nothing but themselves, and would be so whether or not I talked about them. I cannot appropriate them by my words. They are not susceptible to metaphor. They were her breasts, and like no other's, and offered to me, and to no other.

What I can say is that her skin goose-pimpled a lot at first, due to nerves and a central heating fault, and that it wore a combined smell of two days without a wash and some kind of heavily scented soap-powder: elsewhere, even inches away, she smelt entirely different. This breast-smell of clean pullovers and mellowed flesh comes back to me from time to time, but never when I call it: I cannot smell it now, though I can remember what it smelt like at the time. It did not smell as it was doubtless supposed to look, that is like alabaster, a somewhat unfashionable but nonetheless still insidious metaphor for female flesh. The man who first spoke of skin as alabaster must have been looking at it through a telescope, or, rather, through a language, an infection. Who would wish to bed a statue? Has marble ever kissed back? Does stone stick sweat on sweat? And what of the obligatory pedestal? Is it removable? Please Detach From Object Before Intercourse. Replace With Care After Use. No: no face was ever chiselled, no flesh-curve ever sculpted, no woman's body ever made by man. No ideal form has ever had an orgasm. Goddesses gather dust in museums, they are overlooked in art galleries, and catalogued in libraries. I cannot even hint a headshake of regret. I love Marion, and I could rip the universe apart with this piece of information. If, that is, the universe were to display the slightest interest in my little, smudgy, and entirely human passion.

Dear Tom,

In my first year at university I lived in a modern hall of residence. It was an architectural joke, i.e. not funny. Its structure was entirely geometrical, barring the odd nook and cranny which the imagination could quickly knock into shape; a system of perfect cubes laid side by side in blocks around an inner quadrangle, with all four floors identical. It was like a Lego building designed by a computer. You could go and visit a friend in the same block and forget that you had ever left your room, since the decor was uniform throughout: it was a question of whether you had a blue carpet or a brown one, and after a while you lost your eye for this distinction. Moving around the building was a dream of blue-grey walls and mustard doors, and when you got back to your own room it was as if time had stood still there, awaiting your return. The sense of incarceration was utter, but rendered all the more cynical by the flimsiness of the fabric of the building, so that you had the impression of being trapped inside a paper box: knowing that your neighbours lived and breathed in adjacent boxes made you want the paper of your walls to be really strong. It was a monument to prefabricated thought, of which we were getting a lot at the time, but it did breed a certain feeling of brooding solidarity amongst the inmates; the boxy people; the L.E.A.-assisted rabbits in their poster-plastered hutches.

The windows of each room were large and faced onto the central court, so that when you looked out you saw the people in the room opposite looking out at you: the first week's cheery waving was soon replaced by bar-room gossip, not so cheery but far more energetic. The outer shell of the building consisted of concrete trying to look like stonework, or possibly even stonework trying to look like concrete, I could never tell. It was totally grey, bland and chill; and the bursar-red curtains with their optimistic orange checks just oppressed in a different way. Plus February plus essay crisis equals depression times two. My next door neighbour was a jazz musician who played records all day long, bought the course books, and propped his acoustic bass in the corner of the room: I was awed by the length of his fingers and by his ability to reason himself out of working. I quickly learnt to handle the names of Miles Davis, Mingus and Bird not only with cool but also with a lousy Bronx accent; and looking out onto that courtyard with a battleship sky and a sax crying quietly in the door, it was the saddest place I have ever lived.

At night you could hear footsteps transporting their conversations along the corridor outside: snatches of different accents; a laddish belch; the laughter of an unidentifiable number of voices; an occasional scream of hysteria stay out of it yes best stay out of it. I would lie there, thinking about the people in the rooms around me and becoming increasingly obsessed by the total geometry of the building. I would imagine everyone lying in bed, like dead goldfish, and then mentally whisk away the structure of the building, leaving a perfect three-dimensional pattern of suspended sleeping bodies, feet all pointing the same way. The idea was made all the more resonant by the fact that the centre of the courtyard sported a square goldfish-pond, a scaled-down symbol of the building itself, provided by Mr Wit the architect. Of course my idea was not only fanciful, it was inaccurate, I know: for some of them contained more than one goldfish. My bed was an entirely orthodox goldfish-bed: I lay and listened to the footsteps, spawning fantasies about the mermaid who one night would knock upon the door.

Dear Tom,

Before I take this discussion any further forwards, I must first take my memory backwards, or rather move backwards into my memory and uncage three particular incidents.

The first was when I was six. I was staying with my aunt, and playing in the garden with my cousin Nancy, who is five months younger than me. We were playing rounders, insofar as it is possible for two people to play rounders, using a slightly deflated red football and a light blue plastic baseball bat which said "Thunderbat" in raised letters on its curved side. I was batting, and attempting to demonstrate the superiority of the male, which was a silly thing to do because I was no good at games as a child. After a couple of embarrassing misses, which I attributed to foul play on Nancy's part, I connected with the ball and sent it rocketing over the hedge, over the lime tree, over the clouds to land, on completion of its glorious and totally unexpected arc, in next-door-but-two's delphiniums. Surprised, heroic, totally satisfied, I exclaimed "Fuck!" The word echoed across the bland suburban skies, tree-leaves hissed applause, the earth was not far from shaking. Nancy stood stunned into a silence which I took to be admiring. I have no idea where I got the word — from school, I suppose, or graffiti in the street. But as far as I was concerned, the word was born when I said it, and I was reborn with it, expanding into gigantic maturity in the course of one tremendous second.

Nancy, unable to compete with my uncompromising assertion of masculine potency, ran inside and told her mother what I had said, the bitch. But my aunt is a sensitive woman, and who knows, perhaps a coward, so she did not reprimand me directly but instead sent Nancy Pantsy back out to crow a message at me: "Mummy says you mustn't say that word

because it's rude and naughty and only dirty old men say it."
My moment of triumph, which had been ebbing as I pondered
Nancy's disappearance into the house and the inevitable
repercussions of the football in the delphiniums, died. I was
not sure what Fuck meant, nor what dirty old men did, nor
why boys couldn't say things that grown-ups said, but the
blood rushed to my face and my cheeks sprouted fur; my back
hunched, my teeth yellowed, and I dribbled thick saliva. I was
totally, totally ashamed by the word which now lined my
mouth. I bit on the taste.

My next memory lasts one musky and incriminating second.
It must have happened some two years after the dirty
mackintosh incident. I was at a party. I hated parties — I
always got lemon jelly, I could never pin the tail on the donkey,
my parents usually came to pick me up too late. But at this
particular one things were getting pretty wild after an
unusually energetic session of Postman's Knock, and I was
beginning to enjoy myself for once. Suddenly someone
suggested a new game. Looking Up The Girls' Skirts. Screams
of horrified enthusiasm. "How do you play it?" "The boys
have to look up the girls' skirts." (Titters.) "What do the girls
have to do?" "They can do whatever they like, my brother
says." (Red Indian warpath noises. Shrieks from the delighted
squaws.) I had always wondered what went on up girls' skirts: I
had seen my mother in the bath, but I couldn't imagine *that* up
the skirts of any of the girls in my class. I suppose that I
imagined girls' skirts to cover all wickedness, but I could never
match this insistent notion with a visual picture. Now was the
time to find out the truth, and since skinny Joanna Smith was
standing less than a yard away I grabbed her and rammed my
head up her billowing primrose party skirt. Thankfully she
entered into the spirit of things, and stood stock still.

I looked. The white socks and the knees with their funny
rashes I knew about, the thin thighs I suspected, but the heavy,
thick blue knickers reaching all the way up to her waist, this
was something new. There was something so totally blank
about this blue material, so utterly uncompliant, so

containing, that it lent more mystery than any silk or chiffon has done since. It was a visual rap on the knuckles, simple and effective. For years afterwards I saw all the girls in my class housed snug and secret in blue knickers, and even in my sixth form I would regularly turn out to support the girls' hockey XI, to catch from time to time a flash of that intimidating, reproachful, bobbing blue.

My third and last memory is the most difficult to reorganise for you, for it consists of nothing but a smell, pungent, alien and intoxicating; a smell which I shall never smell again but which has revisited me I think four times in the course of eight years, and again, never when I have called it.

It was the smell of my first girlfriend's womanhood, her sex, her perfume. It was the smell of the first rich flowing of her femininity, dribbling and sticky. We were both fourteen; and trying to be a woman, Catherine would cover herself in perfumes, talcs and anti-perspirants; her body was a garden of synthetic delights, of luxury soaps, body splashes, bath salts, lipsticks and powders. I can summon the artifice of her clotted mascara, I can taste the sour rasp of her underarms. I could write reams about that first love, about the first confusing tunnellings of my second finger into the wet warmth of her body, but all that, like the chemist's-shelf she wore to try to make herself a woman, is ancillary, a framework to the main experience which colours my brain and sends cramps shooting through my stomach even now.

After that first uninformed exploration of her body's centre by my aching second finger, her mother arrived in the car to pick her up from my house, where we were supposed to be having tea after our Sunday confirmation class. Catherine got straight into the car, no fond farewells in front of Mummy, and I politely hallo'd and goodbye'd her mother through the open driver's window, my right hand firmly wedged into my trouser pocket. The car, a blue Avenger with a broken tail-light, drove off into the dusk, and waving gaily with my innocent left hand, I lifted that second finger to my nose and inhaled a smell so deep and sharp and present that I nearly wept. And returning to my bedroom, I slammed the door shut, kicked the waste-bin round the floor, threw a few books at the walls, lay down upon the damp-stained bedspread and wept with joy, thanking God for this confirming miracle.

These three memories are linked by more than just their echoing insistence in my mind, though that in itself is enough to link them to each other and to my deathbed: they share a common currency, for they are all losses of virginity, though of entirely different denominations. Virginity is neither a woman's preserve nor her curse, it does not consist solely in the breaking of an obscure membrane by a short blunt object attached to a scot-free male. Virginity denotes presexual innocence, and that innocence is not translated into a state of experience simply by the first painful acceptance of the penis by the vagina, for sex does not consist of just this physical act: sex exists in language, in thought, in images, sounds, tastes, smells, and whenever for the first time one of those modes of sexual identification breaks in upon the innocent sensibility, then a virginity is lost. And, like the broken hymen, the wound once made can never be repaired.

Dear Tom,

The greatest theoreticians are of course not always the greatest practitioners, even of their own theories; and whilst my virginities fell like ninepins as I moved through my teens, the central tower did not fall for all my storming, chivalrous or otherwise. The hymen, I knew, was not always easy to break: to me it took on the aspect of the Berlin Wall, dominated by the machine-guns of my own ineptitude. This was particularly demoralising during my first year at university: I had regarded acceptance into a B.A. Honours course as a passport to sexual promiscuity: it turned out to be a passport to university. I remember reading a student publication which claimed that approximately 40 per cent of students would leave the university after three years without having had intercourse on the premises, and this statistic became a kingpin of my thought: on a good day I would class myself as a sixty man, on a bad day as a forty mouse. The rest of the campus I similarly classified according to their rôles as sixty or forty percenters: inside information on such a large group being scarce, I formed my conclusion mostly from careful observation. Opening line: "Did you know that if you put a couple of sixties together the introduction of a horizontal plane facilitates a 120 per cent passion rating?" In fact I did have a couple of mermaids knock on my door, but they were not my type: not to be deterred, however, I headed for the bed and put my trust in my powers of mental alteration. In this way I managed to waste my time, hurt some people, anger more, and confirm my status as a useless statistic.

My next door neighbour Chas and I would have conversations leaning out of our respective windows and eyeing up the goldfish-pool, talking like New York taxi drivers with laryngitis:

—Hey Chas, you know the accumulation of frustration situation is reaching critical proportions. Unless I have immediate guarantees of its imminent defusal I may have to take evasive action, like the next train home.

—You're not kidding. I did the I Ching last night.

—Whaddaya get?

—Accumulation through restraint, number twenty-six.

—No kid?

—Yeah. Said I have to cross the great water. Whaddaya think that means?

—Means you take a dive into the goldfish and cool off.

—Sublimation, it's my one remaining hope. I mean, look at Edmund Spenser, you wouldn't wanna class him as a Leading Sixty, would you?

—You wanna look at Edmund Spenser?

—I *haven't* looked at Edmund Spenser. Apropos did you know that . . .

—Spenser's poetical works, ya, ya, they told me already. Anyway, the text is primarily a sexual process, ask any structuralist shmuck. I've been reading Roland Barthes, he says the text desires me.

—You try telling that to a medievalist you'll get a face like a trashcan.

—Whaddaya mean? I'm irresistible.

—Yeah, well, Piers Plowman has been resisting me all week.

—That's why you didn't write the essay, right?

—You got it.

—But Chas baby, you're such a warm person.

—That's what I tell everyone. Hey, how d'ya rate the chances of a meaningful encounter between Rosemary Jilks and me?

—How meaningful?

—Pretty.

—Rosemary Jilks, that's the one with the split skirt and the boyfriend in the rugby team?

—She got a boyfriend in the rugby team?

—Looks like he eats six-packs for breakfast. I would rate your chances at an optimum potential of nil.

—Ah! That's the way the daydream crumbles. Reckon I better stick to jazz.

—With fingers like that, you're in your element.

—Ya, well, I need the groupies. Altogether, now — What ain't we got?

—We ain't got dames. . . .

Dear Tom,

When Marion came, I had my head inside the central heating system. It was half-past midnight and the heater had packed up, so I unscrewed the front with a twopenny bit and poked around inside it, completely ignorant of how warm air radiators worked. My fringe was fringed with dust, I had a speck in my eye, and I was half-wearing a pair of baggy dungarees which I had been attempting to mend without taking off when the central heating crisis arose. My underpants, a Christmas present from my mother, are best left out of it.

She knocked and entered the half-open door. She had come, she explained, on the offchance that. I did not press for explanations but did mental Tarzan-swings and yodels: I had desired Marion for months and had had her once already in my sleep, a straightforward but electric union which had launched a thousand orchestrated fantasies. I felt that I exuded lust, a wolf in clown's clothing, so I tried to act in a welcoming and friendly fashion whilst attempting to salvage a modicum of dignity from the wreckage of my heater and the swathings of my dungarees. I organised coffee with great heartiness and explained in detail my new hillbilly approach to things. Did she want jam on digestives? I had strawberry and apricot. Jam on digestives? Yes, you plaster digestives with as much jam as they will take and eat them really fast before they disintegrate all over your lap. It's like cheesecake without the cheese, and habit-forming. She would have jam on digestives. I bombed the bedcover with strawberry jam and shrugged it off, one of life's little trials. Would she like a record? She would. Did she like jazz? She did. I had a friend who played jazz, she must meet him. She would love to. Yes, he was really tremendous. I put *Birth of the Cool* on very quietly because of the hour, then got increasingly agitated because I wanted to impress her with the bass response of my new speakers. I explained the bass response of my new speakers. She was impressed, but appreciated my concern for the rest of the community. Would she like to go and hear some jazz? She would. She would? Then I would have to find out somewhere where they played it, ha ha. Was she cold, by the way? No, no. I demonstrated my mandolin, you can get round-backs and flat-backs, this is a flat-back, you can always tell them because they look like frying-pans. I explained the problems I was having with the bridge. She sympathised. It was a very beautiful instrument. Yes, it was a very beautiful instrument, bugger to play but very beautiful. Would she like another coffee? Could she? Well, of course. Only if I was sure. I was sure. She didn't want to disturb me if I had work to do. No, no, she wasn't disturbing me at all, I was a night owl, I liked to have a good look at my insomnia before tackling it, ha ha. I made more coffee. What did she think of the course? No, let's not discuss the course, she hated it. Fine. In particular she disliked the compulsory medieval paper. On what grounds? She found the medieval attitude to women despicable. Ah. It was a nauseous fabrication, this ideal version of woman in a society which treated women as possessions. Yes indeed. I had a friend who disliked medieval as well. What was most sickening was that their attitudes still prevail in our society, the woman is still an object for male possession, but instead of being entombed in an ideal of perfection she is now kept in check by a leash of totally theoretical freedom. Right. Right. Had I read *Ways of Seeing*? No. Had she read *The Franklin's Tale*? No. Ah. I really liked the pullover she was wearing, it looked like such a soft material. Yes, it was, she bought it in Scotland. It was lovely — could I feel it? Yes, of course. My word, it really was lovely. Was I sitting on her skirt? No, it didn't matter at all, it needed a wash and press anyway. I hated laundry. Yes, laundry was terrible. We never did it. I had seen her in the street the other day and had called across to ask her if she'd like to come and have a cup of coffee somewhere, but she hadn't seen me. Really? No. Where was this then? Outside the post office, she was going into the supermarket. Oh what a pity, she would have loved to come, she wasn't doing anything special at the time. Would she like to go tomorrow? We could have chocolate cake over the road. Chocolate cake? Yes, they did a brilliant chocolate cake with artificial cream, I sometimes had it for breakfast. Oh well in that case, yes, if I wasn't busy. Oh no I wasn't busy, I was never busy. Well, we must go on then. Yes, let's — how about the morning? We could have breakfast. Breakfast? Well OK then, she had always wanted to try chocolate cake for breakfast. Should I change the record? No, I shouldn't bother, we didn't want to disturb anyone this late at night. Right. Was she cold, by the way? Well, a little bit. Had she heard the wide-mouthed frog joke? She had. A blow, that, it was my one clean joke. But she wouldn't mind hearing it again. I told the wide-mouthed frog joke, with all the actions. She collapsed with laughter sideways onto the pillow. I took the opportunity to collapse with laughter sideways on top of her. I was careful to say nothing about her pullover matching her eyes, or any of that crap. She was careful not to move or demonstrate any signs of anguish. I said nothing. She said nothing. Still I said nothing. Still she said nothing. There was soft down on her face which the lamplight sheened into individual golden hairs, and her mouth was half-parted, it was opening. I responded with glimpses of teeth. We forgot about the central heating. I had pins and needles seeping from my elbow to my wrist, I loved it. Her eyes flicked out of contact, back, away, and back again. Whatever you do, shut up, kid. Could she stay the night?

Dear Tom,
   Given that Marion had lost the front light from her bicycle and lived a good three miles out of town, how could I say no?

Dear Tom,
   I started by talking facetiously about moss and melons so as not to talk about them seriously now. I threw mud at alabaster so as not to be blinded into seeing it take shape where it never existed. For nothing that I experienced in that first union had anything in common with the dialects of sex which our culture has evolved; and were I to force those distant minutes onto the typewriter through a sieve of seductive metaphor, chaste or fruity, I would be creating nothing more than yet another glib addition to a literature which has gossiped itself to death already. If the truth be told I remember very little of that first union, fragments simply, like the double smell of Marion's breasts, and as it recedes in time it becomes increasingly interchangeable with the dream which prefigured it. What I do remember is a feeling of utter exposure of which I had no fear, a nakedness beyond flesh which showed my organs beating and my muscles stretching and my white bones grinding wetly; a total recognition of myself in all my blood and breath and

199

marrow; a discovery of my own identity manipulated by the paradox of an uncontrolled surrender to another person, this accident of flesh and spirit whose insides I could not see as yet but only guess at from their desperate pressing at mine. I felt that for the first time I was home, and more than home, no longer lost, in this strange place belonging to another whom I did not know. That loss of loss, that last thick hymen breaking is the sharpest wound of all, for it is absolute but temporary; soon your skin will grow back tighter with a new, more expert pain.

Dear Tom,

Do you want to know who Marion is, this girl who so far is scarcely more than a name that I have spoken? Shall I scribble a portrait in the margin, or compose a paean of praise, or rough out a character assassination? Shall I make her what she is not by trying to make her what she is? I cannot make her anything, she is not mine and I could never make her mine by writing her.

Nor can I explain why it should be Marion, and not some other. The next day she lay a captured mermaid in the sudded backwaters of my bathtub, debunking the entire image by eating fish and chips. I war-whooped my way around the echoing bathroom, sticking chips like feathers in my hair and breaking off occasionally to scrub once more her pristine back. "Why me, idiot?" she said.

Why me, idiot?

Dear Tom,

At the start of the following academic year I stood in that central courtyard looking up into my old room. I could glimpse a different range of posters on the wall, a blouse hanging up to dry, a pink geranium on the window-ledge. A girl's head bobbed above what I took to be a kettle, then disappeared from sight. I wondered if the ghost of our first union haunted that now different room and gasped upon the bed at night, its presence indicated by no more than one of many mattress-stains. In each of the utilitarian cubes that form this strange hotel there must be some such memory lingering, all unknown to the new guest, the new king of the tiny foursquare castle, who lives and seeks to make his own ghosts there. Or perhaps I am indulging in fantasy again, as with my goldfish-scaffold, and your psychic representatives are packed up with the rest of your student clutter at the end of each year. Certainly as my second year progressed that court became increasingly a place to walk through joining A and B. If so, the ghost of our first union simply weeps from time to time in our own two memories, and hovers silent near these pages, unimprisoned by the careful type.

Dear Tomcat, Tomahawk, Tom o'Tales,

I ask but this: why do you have to tap and sweat to teach yourself what you already know? Why fail like this to trap your ghost inside the network of your careful typeface? Why bother, my friend?

Or is it that the spectre of your last virginity has more than one voice, another which you cannot make to speak?

BIOGRAPHICAL NOTES

Neal Ascherson was born in Edinburgh in 1932, the son of a naval officer. He won a scholarship to Eton, and went to Cambridge. He was Scottish politics correspondent of *The Scotsman* from 1975-79, and now works as a freelance contributor to that newspaper and *The Observer*.

James Baldwin was born in Harlem in 1924. He is the author of six best-selling novels, the latest of which is *Just Above My Head*, and several collections of essays. He is the recipient of numerous honours, awards and literary fellowships.

Christine Bold is currently completing a Ph.D. on popular western fiction at University College, London.

George Mackay Brown was born in Orkney. He is the author of two novels and several books of verse, short stories, essays and a play. Several of his stories have been filmed for television.

Ron Butlin is the author of a collection of poems, *Creatures Tamed By Cruelty*. His short stories have appeared in many magazines and anthologies.

Rick Cluchey is the author of a play, *The Cage*.

Jack Debney was born in Cheshire in 1941 and studied English at Leeds University. He was a lecturer in English at the University of Alexandria and since 1970 has been Lektor in the Englisches Seminar at Marburg, West Germany. "The Crocodile's Head" belongs to a sequence of stories set in Egypt.

Gordon Donaldson taught at Edinburgh University for thirty-two years as Fraser Professor of Scottish History and Palaeography. His books include *The Scottish Reformation* and *Scotland: The Shaping of a Nation*.

Douglas Dunn was born in 1942 in Renfrewshire. His books of poems include *Barbarians* (1979) and *St. Kilda's Parliament* (1981) which was awarded the Hawthornden Prize.

John Fowles is the author of four novels, the most recent of which is *Daniel Martin,* a collection of short stories, and a book of "personal philosophy", *The Aristos*.

Giles Gordon was born in Edinburgh in 1940 and now lives in London with his wife and three children. He is a literary agent and edits *Drama*. He has published novels and collections of short stories.

Gerald Mangan was born in Glasgow in 1951. Awarded S.A.C. bursary for poetry in 1978, later held S.A.C. Fellowship as writer-in-residence at Dundee College of Art. Currently reviews fiction for *The Scotsman* and contributes to numerous magazines.

Allan Massie is the author of three novels, the latest of which is *The Death of Men*. He is the present editor of the *New Edinburgh Review*.

Brian McCabe was born in Edinburgh in 1951. He has published two collections of poems and his short stories have appeared in magazines and anthologies. He has given public readings of his work in Scotland.

Norman MacCaig has published many collections of poetry, the latest of which is *The Equal Skies*.

Henry Miller died in 1980 at the age of eighty-eight. He was the author of many books, including *Tropic of Cancer, Black Spring* and *The Colossus of Maroussi.*

Naomi Mitchison was born in Edinburgh in 1897 and is still writing, with one new book coming this year and another early next. She was at one time a competent field botanist with some knowledge of African and Asian flora.

Tom Nairn is the author of *The Break-up of Britain.*

Peter Porter has published several collections of poems, the latest of which is *English Subtitles*. His *Collected Poems* will be published by O.U.P. in 1983.

Sean O'Brien's first collection of poems, *The Indoor Park*, will be published by Bloodaxe Books in 1983. He is represented in the anthology *A Rumoured City.*

Jonathan Steffen is the recipient of a Harper-Wood Literature Studentship, awarded by St. John's College, Cambridge.

James Young is a member of the Department of History, Stirling University. He is the author of *The Making of the Scottish Working Classes.*

Don Watson lives in Victoria, Australia. He is the author of a biography of the Australian journalist Brian Fitzpatrick, and is at work on a biography of Alexander MacMillan.